D0288674

DECIDING TO THRIVE

LESSONS LEARNED IN MY SEARCH FOR THE MEANING OF SUCCESS — AND HOW TO SUSTAIN IT

JOHN WASSERMAN

© 2015 by John Wasserman
All Rights Reserved

Deciding To Thrive: Lessons Learned In My Search
For The Meaning Of Success, And How To Sustain It
Copyright © 2015 by John Wasserman
john.wasserman@me.com
(215) 343-9102

All rights reserved under the Pan-American and
International Copyright Conventions.

No part of this book may be reproduced in whole or in part, scanned,
photocopied, recorded, distributed in any printed or electronic form,
or reproduced in any manner whatsoever, or by any information
storage and retrieval system now known or hereafter invented,
without express written permission of the publisher, except in the
case of brief quotations embodied in critical articles and reviews.
Please support authors' rights, and do not participate in or encourage
piracy of copyrighted materials.

Copies are available at special discounts for bulk purchases in the
United States by corporations, institutions, and other organizations.
For more information, please contact the publisher.

Editorial, production, and publishing services provided by
Winans Kuenstler Publishing, LLC
93 East Court Street
Doylestown, Pennsylvania 18901
(215) 500-1989
www.WKPublishing.com
Cover design by Sherwin Soy
Printed in the United States

ISBN-13: 978-1514333433
ISBN-10: 1514333430

1 2 3 4 5 6 7 8 9 0
First Edition

DEDICATION

To my first two customers, Karin Renner (aka Mom)
and John Wasserman, Sr. (aka Dad),
for always believing in me
no matter what was going on in my life.

A PORTION OF THE PURCHASE PRICE OF THIS BOOK WILL BE DONATED *to support the local programs of Children's Dyslexia Centers, Inc., a network of fifty nonprofit offices in thirteen states that provide tutoring and training services for familes with children affected by dyslexia, an inherited but treatable condition that affects how people learn to read, speak, and process numbers. Famous dyslexics include Thomas Edison, Winston Churchill, Leonardo DaVinci, and Walt Disney. Dyslexia affects about one in five children, boys and girls equally, and if left untreated is the primary reason teenagers drop out of school. It contributes to juvenile delinquency, and puts children at risk of underachieving their potential as adults. Early professional help greatly increases a child's chances of living a normal, fully functional life. For more information, visit: ChildrensDyslexiaCenters.org.*

TABLE OF CONTENTS

Acknowledgements. i
About The Author iv
Preface vi
Chapter 1: In A Golden Rut 10
Chapter 2: The Synthesis Of Happiness 24
Chapter 3: Making Waves 36
Chapter 4: Dragons And Magic Swords 52
Chapter 5: The Sixty Second Rule 64
Chapter 6: Legacy Versus Currency 76
Chapter 7: Is This A $1,400 Day?. 94
Chapter 8: About The Money Thing 106
Chapter 9: Money, The User Manual. 116
   1) Create a Written Game Plan 117
   2) Act Your Wage 118
   3) Get and Stay Out of Debt. 118
   4) Save Yourself 120
   5) Invest In Yourself 121
   6) Invest In Other Things. 123
   7) To Incorporate Or Not Incorporate . . 124
   8) Everyday Insurance 125
   9) Your Community 125
Chapter 10: My Year Of Reading Book List . 128
   Also 138
The Fifty-First Book: Final Thoughts 142
Appendix: Additional Resources 144
   Great TED Talks 144
   Dyslexia Resources. 145
   Additional Reading On Money, Finances . . 147
   Other Recommended Books. 147
   Financial Websites 148
   Overall Financial Advice 149
   Help Managing A Budget 149
   Help Reducing Debt And Saving 150
   Impulse Spending, Building Credit 151

ACKNOWLEDGEMENTS

Darren Hardy, publisher of *Success* magazine, compares writing a book to "riding a roller coaster without the safety bar. Horrific. Perilous. Painful. Endless. Then just when you think it's finally over ... the death drop occurs: editing. Aaaaah!"

I feel your pain, brother. After publishing my first book, *No Shorts, Flip-Flops, Or Sunglasses: How To Get And Make The Most Of Your First Real Job,* I thought, man, never again. But here we are. And without the support of some amazing people this book would still be just an idea.

To the many mentors I had in Vector Marketing Corporation, I am forever grateful. Without the lessons I learned in over two decades with some of the best leaders on Earth and the inspiration you've blessed me with, I can't fathom the path I may have traveled.

Special thanks to the world-class leaders of Vector Marketing Corporation and CUTCO Cutlery Corporation. Thank you all (CEOs, Regional, Divisional, and District Managers) for creating not only a product that is built to last, but a company that is as well. It is a company that cares about everyone from the production line to the sales team and provides its people with unlimited opportunities for personal, professional, and financial growth.

To the Alumni; to those that I have personally mentored over the years at Vector and through Leadership Academy, Branch Preps, "Bootcamps," staff meetings, and one-on-ones: I am thankful for our friendship. I have learned as much from you as you have from me. Thank you for challenging me to bring my best every time. I'll never forget the amazing Limo Nights we shared and exotic trips around the world.

To the book team: Thank you, Raquel Pidal and Foster Winans. You are both kind and patient and super talented at what you do. I am a lucky person to have been able to work with you, but more importantly get to know you.

To our amazing children, Jack and Anastasia: You are smart, talented, good looking (runs in the family), but most of all hard working. Thank you for the fifty hand-crafted bookmarks to show your support for my journey and for all the laughs along the way. I couldn't have done it without you.

And most importantly, to my best friend, my lovely and beautiful wife, Gitana: Thank you for your unconditional love and support. I couldn't do what I do or be who I am without you. You truly are my everything.

ABOUT THE AUTHOR

John Wasserman, an executive with a $200-million-a-year international consumer products marketing company, has coached thousands of people to create indispensable habits for personal and professional growth as they began their journeys to success.

John began his career in 1991 as a sales representative for Vector Marketing, selling CUTCO Cutlery in Philadelphia, Pennsylvania. To date, John has made over $75 million in career sales.

He is CEO of Fast Start, LLC, author of *No Shorts, Flip-Flops, Or Sunglasses: How To Get And Make The Most Of Your First Real Job*, a frequent public speaker, and, as a Division Manager for Vector Marketing, responsible for more than thirty field office locations throughout the Philadelphia–New York metro region. He also maintains a blog on personal and professional growth at JohnsShorts.com.

He and his wife, Gitana, have two children, Jack and Anastasia, and live in the Philadelphia suburbs.

Proceeds from John's speeches and the sales of his books support Children's Dyslexia Centers.

PREFACE

A stack of books changed my life. Fifty of them, to be exact. That's how many I read in a year, one a week. It was a deliberate experiment with an urgent purpose. I had enjoyed a high level of success early in my career only to wake up one day to find myself in a rut, uninspired and drifting.

Those books were the first step in shaking myself out of my professional slump. Reading them helped me make an intentional choice to decide to thrive instead of aimlessly floating, leaf-like, down the river of life.

The completion of that experiment gave me the confidence to write my first book: *No Shorts, Flip-Flops, Or Sunglasses: How To Get and Make The Most Of Your First Real Job*. It is aimed at college-aged men and women who are beginning their working lives and at parents who want to encourage and help them.

The stories and lessons featured in *No Shorts* came from twenty years of recruiting and training young adults to be sales reps for a $200 million-a-year global firm that markets high-end cutlery.

Our business is designed to accommodate students' busy schedules, giving them the flexibility to work part-time or full-time hours around their class and extracurricular schedules. I see my role in their lives—besides teaching them how to sell—as being their first real boss. With that role comes a responsibility to send them on better equipped and skilled for their next job. It can be frustrating at times, but it is never dull. Working with young people keeps you on your toes, and a lot has changed in our technology and culture since I was that age and just starting out, so I feel like I'm always learning something new.

A handful of those young men and women stay with the company, as I did, and move into the role of managers. They run satellite offices where they recruit, train, and mentor people who are just a few years younger than they are. It's a lot of responsibility for someone in his or her early twenties, requiring a great deal of maturity and intuition.

Those office managers are essential to the company's continued success because our sales depend on the thousands of reps we recruit each year to fill slots created when those who have finished their schooling decide to move on or "graduate" from our company to use what they've learned in another field.

After more than two decades of doing this, I decided to write a second book to capture what I've learned about becoming and building great leaders, both from experience and from reading all those books. No matter how clever a title is, or how profound and insightful a book's content is, it turns out there is no secret sauce, no magic bullet, no killer app that will automatically produce leaders who inspire, encourage, teach, and mentor others to become great leaders. Different people respond to different techniques, and in this book, I've compiled a number of them that have worked for me and my teams over the years.

If I had to boil all I've learned down to its essential elements, I might say the kind of person who becomes a good leader in any field likes people and is compassionate, a good listener, and, most important of all, always willing to learn something new and take on a challenge. That was what got me started on this part of my journey and got me to pick up the first of those fifty life-changing books. I thought I knew everything about my job and how to be a leader. I knew I was unhappy, and I'd decided it was time for me to move on.

When I finished that stack of books at the end of the year, I had learned that I didn't know it all by a wide margin, that I enjoyed learning and growing, that I still loved inspiring young people to work toward their goals, and that I got great satisfaction from teaching skills they could use in their careers and in their private lives.

So, let the reading begin!

John Wasserman
Warrington, PA, 2015

CHAPTER 1: IN A GOLDEN RUT

My professional crisis came to a head about five years ago after a good, long run of success. Business in the division I managed had been improving each year and I had become the company's poster child. There had been a string of promotions, sales awards, and free trips all over the world. One year I did so well I won a Rolex watch.

And then my inner flame began to flicker. My group's ranking among the company's divisions slipped. It's not that my best days were over. I was still doing well. But in a large company with a lot of people competing against each other, you can't stay top dog forever. There's a shelf life at that level and it was another person's turn to break all the records.

Once you've been the top dog, losing that status leaves you feeling like your peers are passing you by and, by comparison, you are falling behind. I found myself in a golden rut, looking for the way out.

Doubt cast a shadow on my confidence. Had I lost my touch? Did I peak too early in my career? As my enthusiasm waned, my waist expanded, enough so that my two children started teasing me, poking my stomach and giggling like the Pillsbury Dough Boy. They were cute and funny about it, but I was embarrassed by my weight gain.

I still loved my job and I still wanted to make a difference, to help people grow and prosper, but I was baffled about how to go about getting myself unstuck. What was I doing wrong? Why couldn't I figure this out? Then, after years of positive evaluations, I got a clunker that really stung my self-worth. I felt misunderstood, made up excuses, and considered that maybe I wasn't doing such a great job of concealing my state of mind.

Things were looking bleak when some of my colleagues and I were flown to Chicago one weekend to meet with a leadership development coach. At one point someone  mentioned an old saying that left a big impression: "You can't change how people react to you but you can change how you react to them." I came away from the experience realizing I had to stop making excuses for my misery and take control. But where to start?

It had been years since I'd read a book. It occurred to

me that all the leadership gurus had written at least one and there must be some wisdom to be had by reading a few. If I started reading about business, management, and personal development, I might get some clues to how to fix whatever it was that was broken.

If I started reading, I might get some clues to how to fix whatever it was that was broken.

Goal setting is a big part of sales management, so I made a goal to read fifty books within one year, one a week. Why one a week, and why so many? It seemed like a big commitment for someone who rarely picked up a book and had trouble reading. Although I was not diagnosed as dyslexic, my daughter was.

Dyslexia presented her with challenges in school, but she is in the ninety-second percentile for IQ among her age group, and the diagnosis helped her and her teachers find effective ways for her to learn. I could recognize some of her symptoms as challenges I had faced as a youngster. So I wanted to set my sights high and challenge myself, in part to continue to encourage her in her own educational journey.

The first book I picked was a huge best-seller at the time: *The 4-Hour Workweek: Escape 9-5, Live Anywhere, And Join The New Rich.* That gives you an idea where my head was at the time. The author, Timothy Ferriss, also had a short-lived reality TV show called *Trial By Fire*. In the pilot episode he gave himself one week to try to learn a new skill—the Japanese art of horse archery—that usually takes years to master. He didn't succeed, but it was entertaining and informative watching him try.

 **Life Hack: Any trick, shortcut, skill, or novelty method that increases productivity and efficiency, in all walks of life.**

Ferriss has described himself as an expert on life hacking, which Wikipedia defines as "any trick, shortcut, skill, or novelty method that increases productivity and efficiency, in all walks of life ... anything that solves an everyday problem in an inspired, ingenious manner." I was in a hurry to figure out what to do about my work situation. I needed a life hack.

In the book, Ferriss mentioned that among the many things he'd done in his still-young life (he was barely thirty), one was teaching speed reading. I had always been a slow reader and only grew suspicious of my own dyslexic traits in adulthood. To retain what I read, I had to speak every word out loud (in my head).

The method I picked up that seemed to work best was to skip the first two and last two words of each line of text. The theory is that your eye still picks up those words without having to focus on them, so you still get the meaning of the sentences without getting bogged down.

The message in Ferriss's book that resonated with me was this: "What we fear most is usually what we most need to do." In my case, I had avoided reading because I wasn't very good at it and, because I was a slow reader, I really had to break out of my comfort zone. When I finished his book, I realized I was off to a strong start.

I read everywhere I could—on airplanes, in waiting rooms, in the bleachers at my son's soccer practice. My plan for success involved creating a routine: fifteen minutes of reading in the morning and an hour each night before going to bed. Our children, noticing that Dad suddenly had his nose in a book all the time, wanted to show their support so they began creating bookmarks, making me one for each book.

The second book I read was *Love Is the Killer App: How To Win Business And Influence Friends* by Tim Sanders, a former Yahoo executive. He happened to be giving a lecture to our leadership team around that time, so I got to meet him and tell him about my book-a-week goal.

"After I finish yours, only forty-eight more to go!"

"That's very cool," he said. "I hope you're going to share your journey with others. You know, just as the pleasure we get from owning things is from sharing them with others—our homes, music, food, and so on—the pleasure in acquiring knowledge comes when we share it. That's how we show our love for others."

That struck me as particularly beautiful and wise. I took it to heart.

 The pleasure in acquiring knowledge comes when we share it. That's how we show our love for others.

Later someone shared with me a quote from a book I hadn't yet read but have since. It is a favorite around the world: *Man's Search For Meaning* by Viktor E. Frankl, an Austrian neurologist and psychiatrist who survived three years in Nazi concentration camps, including Auschwitz. In his book he sets out to explain why those who found themselves facing the near-certainty of death and the absolute certainty of relentless misery, deprivation, and despair didn't just kill themselves.

Part of the answer for Frankl and others who survived was to focus on what they could do for others instead of bemoaning their own plight. Among the gifts we can bestow on others, he wrote, is to show others their potential because by doing so we make it possible for those potentialities to come true:

> We who lived in concentration camps can remember the men who walked through the huts comforting others, giving away their last piece of bread. They may have been few in number, but they offer sufficient proof that everything can be taken from a man but one thing: the last of the

human freedoms to choose one's attitude in any given set of circumstances, to choose one's own way.

The more I read, the more I realized that my goal shouldn't be to change who I am, but to become more of who I *already* am—to rediscover myself and build on that. It dawned on me slowly that I was moving in the right direction. Once I got it, I began to put into practice Sanders's advice to me and shared what I was learning with my sales team and with my family. In time, when people came to me with an issue, as they often did, I began to have more thoughtful and helpful responses. I became more credible and reliable as a source because of what I'd been reading.

I became more credible and reliable as a source because of what I'd been reading.

After reading a bunch of books, the titles began to run together. For fun, I drafted a paragraph to see how many I could incorporate.

I got *Inside Steve's Brain, Poured [My] Heart Into It,* learned how to have *Fierce Conversations,* took *The Leap,* studied how to be *Outstanding,* learned *How The Mighty Fall,* how to *Think Better,* what gives us *Drive*, studied *Body Language*, worked to become *The Dream Manager* who was always *Delivering Happiness* and underwent a *Total Money Makeover*, found out *How Successful People Think*, and took notes on *The Last Lecture*. I *Switch-ed*, learned to *Rework*, found *8 Ways To Be Great* only to discover *[I] Already Know How To Be Great*. So I got into a *Tribe* and became a *Go-Giver, The Leader Who Had No Title*.

In time, I developed a reputation as someone who had a lot of practical knowledge and wisdom. "Ask John" became a default answer when there was no other. Invariably, when others came to me for advice, I would have just read something applicable and could then share his or her "ah-ha" moment. This was a big help in leading others, creating a team atmosphere in which it was not only okay to help others reach their goals, it was encouraged. As Frankl concluded in his book:

Success, like happiness, cannot be pursued; it must ensue, and it only does so as the unintended side effect of one's personal dedication to a cause greater than oneself or as the by-product of one's surrender to a person other than oneself. Happiness must happen, and the same holds for success: you have to let it happen by not caring about it.

Success cannot be pursued; it must ensue as the unintended side effect of one's personal dedication to a cause greater than oneself.

As the weeks passed and the stack of finished books grew, I realized I had a thousand great stories and anecdotes that, in retrospect, made perfect illustrations for every one of the issues the authors tried to address. One of the top ten books I read that year was *Becoming A Person Of Influence* by John C. Maxwell.

Maxwell wrote, "The goal of a great leader is to help people think more highly of themselves." When I read that, I thought, That's what I do! That's what I've been doing for almost twenty years. I should write a book!

My first book would be about my company and my colleagues and it would make its points by showing readers rather than just telling them. I wasn't an expert on leadership, but I was an expert on what it's like to learn to be a leader and motivate others. I wasn't an expert on how to school young adults on presentation skills, or write a résumé, or how to keep your dignity in a profane or emotionally unhealthy workplace (such as the third-shift factory job I had one summer where I truly found out the meaning of the term "graveyard shift"). But I had many years of firsthand experience that I could share.

Feeling inspired by the wisdom that was pouring into my head, I decided to risk sharing my dream with a friend.

"You know, I've been reading all these books and I think my next goal will be to write one of my own."

He gave me a sideways look. "Write a book? About what?"

His skeptical response caught me off guard. I should have said, "Yeah, you're right," and dropped the subject. Instead, I started to explain my concept but he remained unimpressed.

"That sounds like a real time suck, and didn't you just say you were concerned about your sales numbers? I don't think you should do it."

That knocked me back a step or two, but it didn't extinguish my desire to write one anyway. But his suggestion that I should focus on my numbers got me reflecting on my golden rut again.

I realized that when it came to my professional life, "Ask John" might work for everyone else, but when I asked it of myself, I was coming up empty. I couldn't see a way out of my stagnant position at work.

The unthinkable began to creep into my thoughts. Find someplace where the grass is greener. Look for another job. Then I read somewhere that "The grass is always greener where you water it."

The grass is always greener where you water it.

It wasn't that I didn't like the company, the work, or the people. I just didn't know how much longer I would have to keep watering the grass before something would sprout. From then on I kept my goals, what I was learning from the books, and my restlessness to myself.

Near the end of my year of books I mentioned to a trusted colleague, someone I had always looked up to, "I think this is going to be my last summer with the company. But I'm going to put my all into it and make sure I go out on top."

My friend was shocked that I would leave after so many years. "Wait a minute! What's going on? Are you kidding?"

Without mentioning my struggle, I said, "I think I'm going to take a year off, maybe write a book."

By the end of that summer, when my performance made it clear that if I were to quit there was no way I would be going out "on top," I was certain I was going to be fired. So I was prepared when one of the senior managers summoned me to a one-on-one meeting, after which we were going to go out and play golf. I was certain it was Doomsday.

After nearly fifteen years with the company, I figured I may as well go out with a bang and I got an idea from an anecdote in *The Accidental Billionaires: The Founding of Facebook: A Tale Of Sex, Money, Genius And Betrayal* by Ben Mezrich. According to the author, founder Mark Zuckerberg was about to meet with some eager venture capitalists who'd made an investment offer. He was going to turn them down, and to emphasize his disdain he showed up in a pair of brightly colored pajamas.

Since we were golfing, not having a sleepover, I put together an appropriate outfit—shorts, shirt, socks, shoes, and visor—of garish, mismatched colors. It got a chuckle, but instead of the much-dreaded evaluation, he said, "Let's just go play some golf. It's a nice day."

It turned out to be one of the best, most relaxed times I'd ever had, and there was no mention of my performance. So when the sun set that night, I still had a job and a decision to make. I could stay and hope to get my mojo back, or I could seek greener pastures.

CHAPTER 2: THE SYNTHESIS OF HAPPINESS

The more books I read, the more I found I was able to give to my coworkers, family, and friends. Some of the books were ideal teaching opportunities, like Stan Slap's *Bury My Heart In Conference Room B: The Unbeatable Impact Of Truly Committed Managers.* (The title is a takeoff on *Bury My Heart At Wounded Knee,* a popular Native American history by Dee Brown published in 1970.)

Stan Slap's book is about discovering your core values, and one of his central messages is that becoming a great leader is a process of trial and error. Unlike scientists, "managers loathe mistakes. [They] are obsessed with results, not blunders in achieving them. Leadership is an equation for making mistakes," he writes. "If you don't screw up your first attempts ... you aren't doing it right. It means you're not moving far enough into new behaviors."

The key to learning from mistakes, he says, is living your personal values at work. In the corporate world, values typically are expressed solely in terms of profit, growth, quality, customer service, and so on. Those, he says, are strategies. Values are something else.

Carl Sandburg, one of America's most celebrated poets (he famously wrote "Sometime they'll give a war and nobody will come"), once observed, "It is necessary ... for a [person] to go away by himself ... to sit on a rock ... and ask, 'Who am I, where have I been, and where am I going?'"

Your answers are clues to your values.

What I found most helpful in Slap's book was the idea that everything we do in life ought to be guided and shaped by our core values, which are unique to each of us. There are a number of workbooks and online resources that aim to help you discover your core values. Stan Slap has a list of fifty to choose from in his book.

I decided to create my own list of core values using the list and exercise in Slap's book. As quickly as I could, and without thinking too much, I began to cross out those that didn't seem like my personal core values. I was able to narrow the list of fifty down to ten, then I thought a bit more and homed in on three that seemed most integral to who I am: work-life balance, innovation, and integrity.

Work-life balance was the most important of the three. I decided there needn't be a difference between my work life and my personal life. I found I liked intertwining both. Now it's what I just call living.

Before this process I was looking for balance by trying to keep everything separate. Now, if I have an event with my company I might have it in my house with my kids and wife present. I love my kids being exposed to the people in my business who, as the years have gone by, are closer and closer to them in age. It's one thing for a parent to explain why certain social and business behaviors are better than others, but nothing educates quite like observation. I hope that they might be inspired by some of my colleagues and learn to be comfortable with people of any age or background.

Innovation as a value means I can't do the same thing over and over again.

Innovation as a value means I can't do the same thing over and over again, hence my fifty-book adventure. I came to see my role in the company and among my colleagues as constantly coming up with new ideas and programs.

I'm not trying to be the next Steve Jobs. I could just as easily call it creativity. But innovation resonated with me. It means rewriting my speeches instead of giving the same one over and over. It means writing this second book. It means spending time on things that get me excited about tomorrow.

The value of integrity was modeled by my father, who worked for more than twenty-five years as a wildlife conservation officer in central Pennsylvania, citing the unlicensed and arresting the out-of-season hunters. When you wear a badge, even if it's got a picture of a deer or a fish on it, your friends, family, and community expect you to behave a little better than everyone else—especially in a rural community where hunting is embedded in the culture.

My father was a community leader and I grew up understanding that people were always watching to see if he was living what he preached. My father did and he expected the same of me. This awareness of the spotlight, however small, has been helpful in my business with what many people say is the hardest part of being a good leader. You can't let your standards down for a minute, or play favorites.

When I went to college and needed to work to pay expenses, I had a part-time job as a dispatcher and guard for the campus police. That gave me stature among my friends and a flirting advantage with the girls, but it also was a responsibility. I had to rein in some of my natural youthful instincts.

Over the years I've worked with thousands of college students and watched how they made the transition between the college jungle (think *Animal House*) and the office, which is more like a zoo with many different personalities having to work together in a confined environment. Many students go into the zoo thinking they're still in the jungle. The office chit-chat tends to be about how hard they partied last weekend and where they're going to be partying hard next weekend. Men and women whose brains are still back in the fraternity or sorority houses will talk about each other using the crude terms that have become commonplace in our culture.

The value of integrity means keeping politics out of the workplace, and resisting the urge to argue with those who don't.

The value of integrity for me means being a leader who never talks that way, modeling language that never, ever includes anything that is foul, demeaning, dismissive, racist, sexist, homophobic, xenophobic, pornographic, intolerant, hurtful, or mean. It means keeping politics out of the workplace, and resisting the urge to argue with those who don't.

New hires who bring any of that jungle behavior with them will quickly figure out what's expected in the zoo and adapt to the standards you set as a leader. By doing so, they will be showing their respect for your values, which you established by not participating in jungle behavior yourself. That's a form of leadership—leading by example—that is authentic and effective.

Because my colleagues and I work with young adults all the time, we feel a special obligation to set good examples. According to some of my peers, it's the hardest part about being in a leadership role—always being "on" for the troops. A common situation comes up during our periodic regional sales meetings where hundreds of reps get together in a hotel to hear inspirational speakers, learn about new products, see who won the sales contests, and of course, check each other out.

The reps range in age from eighteen to about twenty-four. When the work day is done and everyone has time to relax, there are always groups of the over-twenty-ones who head for the hotel bar. We managers and leaders try to have fun during the work sessions and bond with our people. Often some of the young reps will invite one of us to go have a drink with them, the same as they might ask a coach or a teaching assistant at college.

My answer is one version or another of: "I'm here to work with you guys and be at my best, so I want to make sure I stay sharp and set a good example. Thanks anyway." How's that for a buzz-killer!

Sometimes we higher-ups really want to go out with our troops, loosen up, and let them see a bit of our inner child. But ironically, doing so undermines our credibility. They might like us better if we let our hair down with them, but leadership is not a popularity contest.

The process of choosing core values is not a science.

The process of choosing core values is not a science. In fact, it's better if it's done quickly, in about fifteen minutes or so. That's how I do it with the people who work with me. It's a timed event because it's supposed to make you think instinctively, to reveal what your gut tells you. I've done this with many people, having them dive right in and then tell me how they feel about it. It almost always has a profound effect on their outlook and self-image.

This phenomenon has been studied by psychologist Daniel T. Gilbert, a Harvard professor whose specialty is deconstructing how humans define and create feelings of happiness. In one of the most popular TED Talks ever presented, "The Surprising Science of Happiness," Gilbert used a number of examples to show that the fewer choices we have and the less time we have to make them, the happier we are with the choices we make. I suggest that you check it out online, as it's worth a watch.

On the extreme end, a man who had served thirty-seven years in jail for a crime he didn't commit told reporters after he was released that his incarceration had been a "glorious" experience. Gilbert calls this "synthesizing happiness," by which he means we humans have a native instinct to make the best of what we have, and a tendency not to agonize over what we cannot have. Another way this has been expressed is called the tyranny of choice. The more options we have, the less happy we are with the choices we've made. We worry that we could have done better.

When I was in college, before I joined Vector Marketing, I had a very specific dream that I thought was unique at the time but probably was shared with tens of thousands of others. I would earn a degree in management science and get a job running a hotel on the beach somewhere, living rent free, meals included, driving a Porsche—a postcard picture of success.

That was what I imagined—having a big house, living on the beach, making a hundred thousand dollars a year (this was before twenty years of inflation!). I don't remember why I wanted to make a lot of money but probably I would have said back then that it was so I could buy more stuff, or better stuff. I wasn't unhappy, but I don't think I knew what it meant to be happy.

My choices were essentially unlimited and so was my ambition. That sounds like the American Dream, but for many people it's a nightmare because they will agonize over what is the "right" choice and then ever after second-guess the choice they didn't make. I should have taken that other job. I should have stayed with that girl I was dating. I should have bought the red car instead of the blue one.

In his TED Talk, Professor Gilbert said his research found that someone who wins the lottery and someone who is rendered quadriplegic in an accident are just as happy three to six months later as they were before their good or bad luck. This is the synthesis of happiness—we have the power to create happiness out of unhappy or limited circumstances. That's why an innocent man can come out of jail after thirty-seven years and call the experience glorious.

Gilbert concluded that, "When our ambition is bounded, it leads us to work joyfully. When our ambition is unbounded, it leads us to lie, to cheat, to steal, to hurt others, to sacrifice things of real value. When our fears are bounded, we're prudent, we're cautious, we're thoughtful. When our fears are unbounded and overblown, we're reckless, and we're cowardly."

I wrote a personal mission statement –Think Like A Champion–to run my business on my core values.

When I knew what my core values were, I wrote a personal mission statement that incorporated them— Think Like A Champion—and decided to run my business based on my three values. That means that if you are on my team, integrity is not optional. It means I want to work with people who are innovative, creative, and not just waiting for me to tell them what to do all the time. And I want to have a successful business, but not at the cost of a great personal life. I started communicating what I wanted to everyone and that started to attract candidates who shared those values.

Taking it one step further, for my key people I had business cards made up for each of them with their three core values written on the back. I had mine framed and hung on the wall so everyone can see how important I consider living your core values to be.

Before I began my year of discovery through reading, I was desperately bored. I had stopped challenging myself and wanted to do other things than just run the business. Today I define myself less by work than I used to. And that has affected the rest of my life, even to the music I listen to. I used to listen to what everyone else was listening to. Now I'm likely to challenge myself by trying out some music I've never heard or thought I didn't like and make exciting discoveries as a result.

I used to be very reserved and still am on the inside. But one of the other things I discovered was how to innovate within my personality. For my first book cover, I had a photo taken of myself standing with my arms crossed, looking large and in charge. One day one of my colleagues said that whenever I called him and that picture showed up on his phone he felt intimidated. So I took one of my daughter's hats, a floppy-brimmed straw hat with a pink bow on it, put it on my head, and took a selfie that I sent to him to replace the other one. Playing the fool now and then has turned out to be one of my signature tactics and people love it. Now any chance I can, I do something like that, something I definitely would not have done before.

My journey of discovery (or rediscovery) had so far yielded a framework for my life and I had identified my three core values: work-life balance, innovation, and integrity. The next step was to explore how to put it all into practice and how to use what I'd learned to inspire and motivate my team members.

CHAPTER 3: MAKING WAVES

Paging through the growing stack of books, I became increasingly aware of the life lessons that are all around us but often get drowned out by the daily hustle and bustle of making a living, raising a family, and dealing with life's inevitable curve balls. This revelation came to me suddenly one hot summer day when my bubbly, eight-year-old niece was splashing around in the pool with her older brother and my six-year-old son. They made a gaudy threesome in their kiddie floats—a green horse with pink polka-dots, a bright red tube with a flamingo's neck and head, and an inflatable yellow lawn chair.

We adults—parents and relatives—were engaged in predictable conversations about such things as child rearing and lawn fertilizer when my niece uttered a piercing, full-throated shriek: "LET'S MAKE WAVES!"

The three kids began jumping and bobbing in their floats until the pool surface boiled with waves that sloshed over the walls and raced across the deck. With faint sighs of annoyance, we snatched our towels and books off the pavement ahead of the deluge.

It had been so long since I'd been that age, enjoying a blissful summer day without a care in the world, ready at a moment's notice to provoke some hilarious mayhem just for the thrill of it. A pang of longing squeezed my chest. When was the last time I'd given myself permission to do something other than just going through the motions or doing what was expected? Somewhere along the line I had stopped growing and this, I realized, was a problem I needed to address.

Somewhere along the line I had stopped growing and this was a problem I needed to address.

Of course, there was a book for that, one of the most inspiring I read on the subject—*Mindset: The New Psychology Of Success*, by Stanford University psychology professor Carol Dweck. Her research identified two ends of a spectrum of how we see ourselves and how that self-vision affects our relative satisfaction with life.

At one end there are those who think of themselves as having been born with certain abilities that define their level of achievement in life. Dr. Dweck describes this as having a fixed mindset.

"People with a fixed mindset believe that their traits are just givens," she says. "They have a certain amount of brains and talent and nothing can change that. If they have a lot, they're all set, but if they don't ... So people in this mindset worry about their traits and how adequate they are. They have something to prove to themselves and others."

At the other end are people who believe success results from hard work and self-improvement. These people have a growth mindset. So the obvious question is whether successful people are born or made.

The answer lies somewhere in between. We all know or have heard of someone who seems incompetent yet somehow rises to the top of an organization or achieves some other success, apparently in spite of themselves. On the flip side, there are people who end up broke or out of a job in spite of having been born with extraordinary gifts.

The difference between having a fixed versus growth mindset turns out to be a big deal and learning about it spoke directly to my state of mind. When my enthusiasm for my work began to flag, I blamed it on having been knocked off my perch, no longer the poster boy, the beater of sales records, the guy everyone wanted to be.

In my fixed mindset it was all about the results. If your definition of success is to be number one, failure is inevitable because no one stays number one indefinitely.

When that sense of failure comes, you start thinking that all the effort to get to the top was a waste. Now what?

The fixed mindset is how most of us feel about money when we're young. At some point we carry around a picture of success in our heads that presumes a bulging bank account or secure income. Who doesn't want to be a millionaire? It doesn't matter if you'd spend it on cars and houses, or stick it in your mattress, or give it away, money does make the world go around. But as a culture, Americans are hyperconscious of which step of the economic ladder we're on. Money is how we keep score. We envy or aspire to be one of the wealthy and we pity or even look down on the poor.

"The fixed mindset creates an internal monologue that is focused on judging," Dr. Dweck writes. So if you are failing to meet your fixed mindset about success or money, you tell yourself you're a loser. If you are passed over for a promotion, you might tell yourself you just don't have what it takes to move up. If you have trouble paying the bills, you might think of yourself as a bad provider. If your kid gets in trouble, you're a bad parent.

People with a growth mindset react to positive and negative information as opportunities to learn and improve.

On the other hand, people with a growth mindset react to positive and negative information and developments as opportunities to learn and improve. Her research convinced Dr. Dweck that "People with a growth mindset see their qualities as things that can be developed through their dedication and effort. Sure they're happy if they're brainy or talented, but that's just the starting point. They understand that no one has ever accomplished great things—not Mozart, Darwin, or Michael Jordan—without years of passionate practice and learning."

After a Columbia University survey found that nearly all parents think it's important to tell their kids how bright and talented they are, Dr. Dweck conducted a fascinating experiment to see what effect that message might have on student performance. Her subjects were fifth graders in New York City public schools. Each child was given a puzzle to solve that was easy enough so every student would be successful. At the end of the test, half of the children were praised for their intelligence: "Look how smart you are!" The other half were praised for their effort: "You worked so hard!"

Then the same children were tested again, except this time they could choose between a test that was as easy as the first or one that was more difficult. The results were decisive and telling—nearly all the kids who had been praised for working hard on the first test challenged themselves by opting for the harder test. Those who had been praised for their intelligence the first time picked the easier test instead.

"When we praise children for their intelligence," Dr. Dweck wrote in her study summary, "we tell them that this is the name of the game: Look smart, don't risk making mistakes."

Then Dr. Dweck gave all the children a third test that was designed for seventh graders. As expected and planned for, all failed. The two groups of children—the "smart" ones and the "hard workers"—responded to their failures very differently. The kids who had been praised for their effort on the first test said they failed because they didn't try hard enough. They even went so far as to tell the researchers it was their favorite test.

The smart kids, however, were shattered, worried that  they weren't really smart after all. "Just watching them, you could see the strain," she said. "They were sweating and miserable."

Finally, Dr. Dweck had all the kids given a final round of tests that were as easy as the first, and here the results were shocking. The hard workers improved their scores by about thirty percent. The "smart" children, whose confidence had been undermined, did about twenty percent worse.

Any parent, manager, or leader would have to look at these results and come to the conclusion that the "everybody gets a trophy" theory of motivation is dead wrong. It is, in fact, demotivating, even crippling. People love the feeling that they are growing, improving, getting better. The more they improve, the better they get.

The experiences I was having as a result of seeking growth through reading—becoming a trusted leader and adviser—helped me begin to think of success differently. In the sales and marketing world, we live in what's been called The Tyranny of Now—did you hit your sales targets this month/quarter/year? I made a conscious decision to focus instead on how I could identify and recruit the best candidates to assume leadership roles, believing that in time those all-important sales numbers would follow. It took a year or two, but it worked out just that way.

John C. Maxwell, who became one of my favorite authors during my reading challenge, started his career as a minister and has become a leading management expert. I consumed six of his books and his message was in step with Dr. Dweck's. "You cannot give what you do not have," he wrote. "In order to develop your staff, you must keep growing yourself."

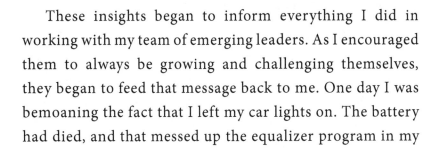

You cannot give what you do not have. To develop your staff, you must keep growing yourself.

These insights began to inform everything I did in working with my team of emerging leaders. As I encouraged them to always be growing and challenging themselves, they began to feed that message back to me. One day I was bemoaning the fact that I left my car lights on. The battery had died, and that messed up the equalizer program in my stereo system. "I can't fix it," I said. "I'm just no good at that stuff."

One of my managers piped up, "I could teach you."

I was about to say something negative about my technical abilities—something from my fixed mindset—but I realized he was challenging me. "Okay," I said. "I could learn." So we went out into the parking lot and he sat with me in my car showing me how to do it.

As a parent, I began to apply what I was learning to my family affairs. Like most of the other parents in my peer group, my wife and I had a tendency to hover—helicoptering—over our kids. That trend is beginning to wane—the new one is called free-range parenting where you let your kids figure things out on their own.

Lenore Skenazy is a New York newspaper columnist and blogger who has been dubbed "America's Worst Mom" for a free-range experiment she did with her nine-year-old son. She gave him a map, a subway pass, and twenty dollars and left him in a department store in midtown Manhattan to find his way home alone. He made it in forty-five minutes, safe and sound, "ecstatic with independence."

I don't know that I would have had the courage to try that myself, but part of my deliberate effort to grow was trying to steer away from telling my children how to behave and do things and instead showing them how to learn. One of those lessons is how to be a good role model. We tell our children that other people are always watching them. Should an opportunity arise, they want to give those other people a basis to believe that if there's an opportunity on the line, they've got a better chance to be chosen.

Part of my effort to grow was trying to steer away from telling my children how to behave and instead showing them how to learn.

But telling them is not the clincher. It's living it. So when we went fishing, I picked up stray trash. They saw what I was doing and began to imitate me. When we travelled, if I saw someone struggling with their luggage on the plane, I was usually the first to offer help. Now they are always alert to opportunities to help someone.

How to deal with adversity was a more nuanced lesson but applicable to everyone at one time or another. One day our kids came home upset about an incident on the school bus. One of the older kids, a neighbor where we lived, had been bullying one of the smaller children. It is a parent's first instinct to protect any kids from being hurt and to scold or punish the person doing the hurting.

My wife and I could have told our children what a bad person this boy must be. We've all heard adults talking about other people's kids as being "a bad seed" or "a troublemaker."

Instead, we asked our son and daughter, "Why do you think he does this?"

"I don't know," they answered, eyes suddenly wide with surprise.

"Well, do you think maybe he's having problems at home? Or maybe his parents aren't getting along? Or maybe somebody is bullying him?"

With those possibilities in their minds, we talked about what to do.

"Tell him to stop being mean," our daughter suggested.

"Yeah, and then he's gonna start bullying you," her brother replied.

Should they tell the bus driver? Maybe, but unless there was a fight or somebody really got hurt, what could he do about it while trying to safely operate the bus?

My wife and I were torn. Did we let the school know, as opposed to discussing it with the boy's parents and risk putting them on the defensive? In the meantime we suggested that our son, who was tall for his age and more of a match for this boy, sit next to anyone on the bus that seemed threatened by the bully. Our son acted as a protector for the smaller kids and even went out of his way to get to know the bully. Not only did the bullying stop, but the two ended up becoming friends. The kids were able to solve the problem on their own without any intervention from us or the other parents.

When our daughter came home complaining that she and her friends spent their recess arguing about which game to play, I suggested that she could be a leader and come up with a solution. "Tell them you'll all play one person's favorite game today, and then everyone else will get their turn each day until everyone's had their chance. And make sure you go last."

I told her about the Marine Corps tradition that at mealtimes the senior officers always eat last, sacrificing their own comfort for the good of their soldiers. In other words, think like a leader and you'll become one. It worked.

I told my daughter, Think like a leader and you'll become one.

Using the lessons I was learning, I saw my daughter in our driveway one day trying to shoot a basketball through the net and getting frustrated. I could have played the cool, knowing dad and showed her some techniques, but instead I asked her, "What do you think happened?"

She rolled her eyes. "Uh, I missed, Dad."

"So, what do you think you need to do differently?"

She thought about it for a second. "I need to throw it higher."

She did, and missed again.

"What did you do that time that you need to do differently?"

A moment of thought. "Lean more forward."

After a few rounds of this, she was making baskets on

her terms. She had taught herself and all I had to do was challenge her fixed mindset that she couldn't make the basket.

Then she threw the ball to me. I took a shot and missed.

She immediately piped up, hands on hips, "So, Dad, what do you think happened there? What could you do differently?"

On the flip side, my daughter is a pretty good artist for her age and one day she drew something that I thought was amazing. It's a natural instinct to praise your child, even if it's for something that isn't all that great. At least she tried, right?

In this case, I really liked it but instead of flattering her I said, "I can tell you put a lot of work into that."

"Yup! I really did." There was a note of triumph in her voice.

"Well, tell me how you did it. Walk me through it. What was the best part? What was the most rewarding part? What do you think about it now that you completed it?"

In the end, she defined her own success. It wasn't handed to her on a silver platter. My questions helped her connect the finished project with the effort that went into it. It wasn't just a picture pinned to a wall or fridge, it was a creation, an expression of who she is, what she thinks, what she likes. In the process of answering my questions, she got to know and understand herself a little better.

Out of all this growth I began to develop a general philosophy to look for the good in every situation. If someone fails to meet their sales targets, it's the same series of questions that begins, "What do you think happened and what could you do differently?" In other words, what can you learn from disappointment or failure as opposed to being critical of yourself or blaming someone else? I might know the answers to every question I ask, but I want my reps to find, and own, the answers. That way they will be more invested in implementing them.

> # What can you learn from disappointment or failure as opposed to being critical of yourself or blaming someone else?

I knew I was getting through to my team when one day I took them all out for a nice dinner at a newly opened steak house that had been recommended by one of my sales managers. He was friends with the owners and wanted to show his support. The place had only been opened a week or so and business was slow. I was game.

The waiter completely forgot to bring my appetizer and the steak was overcooked. I didn't say anything at the time but mentally I crossed it off the list of places to eat out. Afterward the fellow who talked me into going there asked me what I thought. I told him what happened.

He looked crestfallen for a moment, then he brightened and asked, "Do you mind if I tell them you really enjoyed the food?"

I hesitated. But then I realized the restaurant had just

opened and they were probably still ironing out the kinks. It would be something else if the place had been around for years, but I had to ask myself the same questions I asked my kids about that bully. What might have been going on in the kitchen? Was it the waiter's first night? Was I being a bit spoiled and unnecessarily critical?

"Sure," I said. "You can say that, this time anyway." In the year or two since, I've been back at that restaurant dozens of times and the food and service have always been great.

Getting intentional about my own fixed mindset included changing my diet—which was a challenge—and losing the twenty-five pounds that I had gained before my journey of discovery began. That was a big win—growth by shrinking.

One of the little things I changed in my life that had a big impact was no longer using the snooze feature on my alarm clock in the morning. I realized that I had been snooze-bingeing, something most people do thinking they are getting a few extra minutes of sleep. But you don't really rest because your mind is on the next time the alarm will ring and whether you have enough time for one more

snooze. When you finally do get up, you have less time to get ready to leave for work.

Once I quit using the snooze button, I felt better about myself, more in control. In a very tangible sense I was starting off every day with a win. I successfully accomplished the first objective of the day—get out of bed.

The next step in my journey was to figure out how to maintain my newly found motivation and desire to grow. That would end up involving a roll of the dice.

CHAPTER 4: DRAGONS AND MAGIC SWORDS

When it comes to personal well-being and career success—however you define well-being or success—none of us has all the answers and there are no answers that fit us all. BUT there are some common aspects of human psychology that leaders see a lot. Now that I was reading about them in depth in all those books, I began to decode the biggest obstacle most people ever face in life—ourselves. Or, more accurately, the voices in our heads. They're talking to you right now, even as you read. What they're saying may be all that stands between you and your potential.

That was the message in one of the most influential books I've read: Alan Fine's *You Already Know How To Be Great: A Simple Way To Remove Interference And Unlock Your Greatest Potential.* Fine was a professional tennis coach in the UK in the 1970s and today he is a sought-after executive coach and consultant.

What makes him remarkable is that the robust, bushy-eyed public speaker he became started out life as a sickly, withdrawn child with a serious asthmatic condition. With other health issues, the asthma was bad enough that he couldn't play sports and missed about half his elementary school years.

He says he was a skinny, shy eleven-year-old Welsh nerd when his brother, as a prank, signed him up for their school's tennis tournament. He had never played tennis before but showed up for his first match anyway, figuring it would be a quick and merciful elimination. Instead, in spite of his physical limitations and lack of training, he won his way right up to finalist. He said he didn't think much about it: "I just put one foot in front of the other."

Then he met his opponent, a tall thirteen-year-old who was already shaving and built like an athlete—the school's number-one jock. With full expectation he would be slaughtered 6-0, 6-0, Fine kept putting one foot in front of the other until, an hour into the match, he realized that he'd managed to battle the hairy beast to a win in the first set, 6-4, and was way out front in the second set, 4-0.

"Then a voice in my head said, 'Alan, you've already won ten games,'" Fine recalls. "'You only have to win two more and you're the school champion.' And that's when I froze."

Instead of focusing on the ball, he was listening to the voice—only two more, just two more. He totally choked.

"The harder I tried, the worse I got, and the worse I got, the harder I tried. I knew what to do, but I couldn't do what I knew." He lost the next six games to tie the match at one set each, and then lost six more games before dragging himself off the court, wrung out and bewildered. "That started me on my search for what was going on and I quickly realized that that voice was everywhere in my life."

He concluded that most of the time people know what to

do, whether it's how to play tennis, how to be a good parent or dependable friend, how to save money, and so on. But those voices in our heads cause us to doubt or to hesitate or to take unnecessary risks, to surrender to the fight-or-flight response, or to choke when we were otherwise on a roll.

What, I wondered, were the voices in *my* head saying?

Among the many things Fine wrote that resonated for me was the observation that people tend to think that success, happiness, fulfillment, and so on can be achieved if they can just find that one bit of knowledge or reach a certain level of success. Once that happens—once they find the magic sword and slay the dragon—the clouds will part, a golden sun will shine down out of a clear blue sky, and all of their potential will blossom and bear fruit.

Before I started working with Vector Marketing, the possibility that I could sell $10,000 worth of heritage cutlery as a college student while going to school full time was as close to winning the lottery as I dared imagine. That, I was sure, would make me very happy and feel successful. When I hit that goal, I realized $10,000 is no big deal. Lots of other kids all over the country sold as much. But $100,000—now THAT would be something! And so on.

 **The funny thing about money is it always seems that somehow there's NEVER enough.**

That's the funny thing about money. Whether a person is homeless, middle class, or a billionaire, it always seems that somehow there's NEVER enough. Sometimes the accumulation of massive wealth ends up serving good causes. Bill Gates, Warren Buffett, and others who are extremely wealthy have pledged to give their fortunes away. But doing good while doing well can't protect some people from the voices in their heads.

Doing good while doing well can't protect some people from the voices in their heads.

A gruesome example is what happened to Robert W. Wilson, one of the most successful individual investors in the history of Wall Street. Over some thirty years he personally accumulated an estimated $800 million, equal to about a billion dollars today, just trading stocks. He retired at about sixty years old to his massive, sumptuous apartment in New York City, on the sixteenth floor overlooking Central Park, with walls and shelves filled with priceless works of art.

Yet when he went out to have lunch with friends, he often showed up in old chinos that were too short for his legs, shabby out-of-style sneakers, and flimsy nylon windbreakers. He didn't like paying for cabs so he always took the subway. He preached against excessive government spending and then told a struggling acquaintance who'd asked for a $400 loan that he should go to the welfare office "because that's what it's there for."

Wilson had no children, trusted no one, had no close friends, and gradually gave away most of his estate to worthy causes like the New York City Opera. A month or so after suffering a stroke, without so much as a goodbye note, he jumped out his kitchen window. There are a lot of ways to leave this world and Wilson could have had it any way he wanted.

Instead, Robert W. Wilson is now remembered as the crazy old rich guy who'd completely lost his dignity and sense of purpose and made a spectacle of himself on the way out of this world. His tale is proof that success and happiness have no price tags and they aren't destinations. Yet most of us at one time or another chase after those tantalizing mirages, and, as I did, we buy a lot of books looking for answers. By some estimates there are more than 100,000 books listed on Amazon just on the subject of finding your life purpose.

It turns out there is no magic sword. Even if there was, no matter how many dragons you might slay with it, there will always be another waiting to take its place—real or imagined.

So the next stage of my growth became about understanding, interpreting, and getting past the messages in my head that were holding me back. In order to be able to inspire and motivate others, I needed to draw on my inspiration and figure out how to keep myself motivated.

> # To be able to inspire and motivate others, I needed to figure out how to keep myself motivated.

One change I made was deciding to rewrite my sales meeting speeches rather than give the same one year after year. The voice in my head said, "It's a whole new crop of faces each year, so it's all new to them. What's the difference? It's less work for me." But I found it stimulating to think of new anecdotes from my life and the business to make my points. I tried to hone my skills as a speaker and to test out new ideas and tactics to positively influence the agile minds of college kids, some of whom would never forget the few months they spent selling knives and being their own bosses.

My journey through Alan Fine's book helped me focus on one of the biggest problems faced by young managers. They have a difficult time controlling their emotions when bad things happen and staying focused on the things that they can control. Young office managers are chosen from the ranks of reps and they are responsible for setting up their own temporary satellite offices in time for the prime recruiting seasons—summer and winter breaks.

Something always goes wrong. The Internet installation gets postponed a week, which means you can't do business.

Some of these emerging leaders panic and occasionally take out their frustrations on innocent customer service reps after one too many calls trying—and failing—to get their installation appointment. Sometimes the receptionist the manager just hired and spent hours training, after interviewing a dozen people, quits on the third day and now he has to go through the whole process again.

As a seasoned veteran, I've learned the hard way that dragons rarely show up at a convenient time, and you will not be able to kill them all, but somehow you will get past them and the tasks get done. That's basically the history of modern civilization—two steps forward, one step back.

Dragons rarely show up at a convenient time, and you will not be able to kill them all, but somehow you will get the tasks done.

So I've trained myself to give a frustration or disappointment that I can't control a maximum of sixty seconds of grumbling before I turn my focus to fixing whatever's broken and working around what can't be fixed. But to help my young leaders, not yet battle-hardened, regain their focus, I have to do more than just tell them to calm down or walk it off.

One of my young managers, Patrick, was having just those kinds of snafus pop up. With the stress of keeping up with his college studies, I could see he was tuned in to the voices in his head that were holding him back from doing what he knew. He was choking, much as Alan Fine had in the school tennis tournament.

Neither the Internet nor the office telephone was working and he spent four hours with customer service getting it straightened out while his receptionist did the best she could taking calls wirelessly on a borrowed iPad. One dragon after another kept popping up. Despite this, his sales were already running well ahead of the year before and his office team was a sales leader.

One day he got so frustrated that he told me, "I think I'm just going to fire my whole team tonight and start over." He was venting, but did seem ready to fire at least a few people. The big season in our business was just about to start, so it was not a good time to be tearing up the game plan. It was the moment for me to step in, as I was learning to do, with questions rather than answers.

"Let's try something, okay? Let's sit down, and I want you take out a sheet of paper and on it write down everything that's bothering you, every complaint that you can think of, every negative thing that's happened since the summer began."

Five minutes later he had filled the page and looked up.

"All right. I think I've got it all."

"Are you sure?" I asked.

"Yeah. I'm sure."

"Okay, now take that piece of paper, crumple it up, and throw it in the trash can."

He uttered a surprised "Ha!" and shook his head. "After all that work?"

"It's all garbage," I said, "and you need to throw out."

He crumpled it up, tentatively at first, but then he scrunched it into a tight ball and shot a basket into the trash can.

"See? It's all in the past. Now you can focus on the positive. You want to feed hope to your people and get them excited about the future. None of what you wrote down is going to help you do that."

Then we talked about what was working. Sure, he had some lazy reps, but even so his sales were up seventy percent and he admitted that he had some people who were eager to work hard.

"You've got a team meeting tonight," I said. "Instead of ripping into people who aren't doing the job, I want you to spend three to four minutes on every single person that's doing the job well, and I want you to recognize them in front of the whole team. Tell them why they're great, how this is going to benefit their future, why you're proud of them. Then, lead the team in a round of applause for each one."

His eyes lit up and the creases in his brow softened.

"Let people know that if they didn't get recognized, it's only because they missed hitting the minimum sales target. Tell them you really want to recognize everybody at the team meeting the next week, and you really want to see them hit that mark and be recognized, too. Highlight the successes. People will quickly get the message that it's how you get praise here."

He managed to turn himself and his approach around. One of his reps became the top-selling person in the division and one of the leaders in the region. That summer he hit the ball out of the park.

CHAPTER 5: THE SIXTY SECOND RULE

What I preach is what I've learned to practice. When I'm frustrated or not feeling motivated, I write a list of goals for the season, the year, and so on. One recent summer, business was down for the company, for my region, and for me. The numbers were terrible, nowhere near the goals I'd set at the beginning of the season. The roar in my ear was the voice scolding me for not hitting my targets and it was a distraction from doing the work necessary to get back on track.

So one miserable day, I got out the list of goals I'd written, put a match to the paper, and watched it turn to ash in my backyard firepit. Then I sat down and started a new one. I projected new numbers that were realistic and I could be excited about beating. I moved the goal line so I'd have a chance to have a win, even if it wasn't the big win I had hoped for. That exercise remotivated and reinvigorated me. Like Alan Fine, I just put one foot in front of the other and made my way out of my funk.

From the books I was reading, and from my own interpretation of how to implement the ideas, I came up with other techniques for keeping myself from getting wound up or so frustrated I wanted to throw in the towel. As my growth continued, I shared some of those techniques with my junior managers when they'd ask for help, as they increasingly did because I always seemed to have an answer. If you're stumped, the more senior managers would say, ask yourself, "What would John say?"

One day I got this email from one of my newer managers:

"John, for some reason I keep having dreams about my branch failing. Like literally when I am sleeping I dream about people walking out of interviews, no one showing up for training, and all of the negative aspects of running an office. Why?"

 **What happens when golfers worry about hitting into the water? They hit into the water.**

Having learned from and been so influenced by Alan Fine's book, I had a ready answer. I wrote back:

"That's not unusual. It's like golfers who worry about hitting into the water. What happens next? They hit it into the water. But that doesn't mean they're failures as golfers.

It means they hit bad shots.

"Good golfers—good athletes in general—are able to put that stuff behind them and be ready to take their next shot. The best baseball players take a bad-call strike without so much as a peep or a sneer. They don't kick dust at the ump or wave their hands or throw things. They step back up to the plate ready for the next pitch or head to the dugout to wait their next turn at bat.

"You will have people leave your interviews because they don't want the job, but that doesn't mean you're a bad manager. It's not personal. It simply means they don't want the job. You'll eventually learn to put that stuff behind you when it happens, as so many of us have before you."

One way to "put that behind you" is to come up with a word, a phrase, a device—some sort of mantra that brings you back to your center.

One way to "put that behind you" is to come up with a word, a phrase, a device—some sort of mantra that brings you back to your center. One that my wife and I agreed on is the "Sixty Second Rule," which we invoked on our way back from a vacation in South America.

We'd bought four bottles of wine that the security folks would not let us take on board in our carry-ons.

We deliberately did not put them in our checked bags to avoid the risk of any of them breaking. Now, at the last minute, the guards made us repack the wine in our checked bags. We wrapped them in our clothing as carefully as we could under the circumstances, but when we got home and opened the bags we found two bottles broken and all our clothes ruined.

"Geez Louise!" I blurted. "Those jerks …"

"Oh, no!" Gitana, my wife, fussed. "Look at our luggage. It's ruined!"

The Sixty Second Rule, The Silver Lining Corollary, and the So Far, So Good Hypothesis.

The Sixty Second Rule meant we could give ourselves about sixty seconds of teeth-gnashing, name-calling, and lamenting. After that, we weren't allowed to carp or grumble about something that couldn't be undone. We added to the Sixty Second Rule what you might call the Silver-Lining Corollary—every "disaster" or frustration has to have some silver lining. In this case, we had an excuse to shop for new wardrobes. We also had come home with an entertaining vacation story to tell.

Finally, I added on what you might call the So Far, So Good Hypothesis. The title comes from an old joke about a hopeless optimist who falls off the roof of a tall building and as he hurtles toward the pavement, tells himself, "So far, so good!" When you quit listening to the voices in your head, it doesn't take much to get from anger and self-pity to acknowledging that if whatever's got you stirred up is the worst thing that happens to you that day, it'll probably be a great day.

The next step for me was to find a way to remind myself of the rules, corollaries, and hypotheses in the moment, which is hard to do when you're fired up. And how do you keep your focus every day when life moves at such high speed and people are impatient for answers before they even finish asking the question?

As it turns out, the answer can be as simple as a rubber band or one of those colored cause wristbands. When asked, many people will tell you about some  small object or gesture that reminds them of something important in their lives. Someone I know wears a ring worn by his mother because it was a gift she received for helping a starving artist. It reminds him to be generous.

Some people pray, some meditate. I found my touchstone in a drawer at home—a pair of blue dice. I took one and set it on my dresser with the number one facing up. Number one was always my goal. So every day when I get ready to leave for the office, I pick that single die up and set it down. It reminds me to beware of the negative voices and think instead like a champion. I pick it up, tell myself, "Think like a champion today, John," and then put it back down.

I had wristbands made up with the words "Think Like A Champion" printed on them and gave them out to my managers. I invested in having some special dice made up with those words printed on the side with the single dot, and gave them away, too.

Some people I know wear a rubber band on their wrist and when they encounter a tough situation and need to remind themselves of whatever principle or phrase motivates them, they stretch and let it snap against their wrist. A little bit of pain apparently goes a long way in making someone stop and reflect.

One top manager I know always had a toy yak with him that helped him keep his eye on the prize. Some people carry a picture of a relative or mentor, someone they admire or someone they want to make proud. It doesn't matter what it is so long as it becomes as habitual as brushing your teeth.

As managers and leaders, it's our job to inspire and motivate others. I have given away many wristbands to many people, some of whom wear them so long they fall apart and write me asking for a new one. On a higher level, our company, Vector Marketing, recognizes top sales managers by collecting congratulatory letters from their colleagues and putting them together in a bound volume. I've been the recipient of one of those and it gave me a lot of self-confidence and motivation to do even better.

Everything worthwhile that I was learning from my books I've tried to pass on to my team. Some get it, of course, and some don't and move on. There was one fellow who stands out for having gotten it in a big, thoughtful, and totally unexpected way. He and I were having a tough time communicating and were going through a rough patch. We were arguing about petty stuff. All the borrowed wisdom I could muster seemed to bounce off him. He was heated and passionate about his point of view, and I assumed he probably thought I was a jerk.

One day, on my birthday, he walked into my office with a warm smile on his face and handed me a small package.

"Happy birthday, John. I put something together for you. Take a look."

It was a small bound notepad filled with writing. Each page had the date and a sentence or two describing something he appreciated about me. I was blown away by the fact that he'd been doing this all through our rough patch. I've kept that little book nearby as another reminder, like the blue die, of what really matters in life.

This happened several years ago and neither of us mentioned it to anyone else at the time. He mentioned it in a talk for the first time recently. "You're never going to see eye to eye with people all the time," he said, joking that, "some days were harder than others to think of something positive to write."

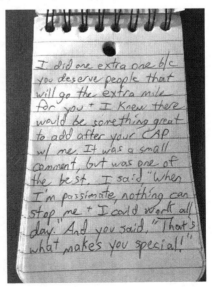

70

The Kill 'Em With Kindness Play: Instead of slaying the dragon, love it to death.

You might call this the Kill 'Em With Kindness Play. Instead of slaying the dragon, love it to death. It's a tactic I had a chance to see in action at a real estate convention in New York. The featured speaker was Donald Trump, so the venue was packed with thousands of people eager to hear words of wisdom from The Donald. Seating was unassigned and an announcer admonished the crowd, "Do not save seats for people who have not arrived."

We were sitting next to a friendly couple from Ohio with whom we hit it off. During a break in the program, the couple went to get some food and asked us to save their seats.

In one of those New York minutes, a middle-aged woman who seemed to have appeared out of nowhere had plunked herself down in one of the Ohio couple's seats. She was clutching in her lap a goodie bag full of real estate literature. She shot us a scowling glare, like a cat guarding its food bowl, saying without words, "I just dare you to try and get me out of this chair. Don't even think about it!"

We started to explain but she cut us off.

"They SAID you aren't allowed to save seats! So I'm not moving!" She settled triumphantly into the chair.

My mind ran through a vocabulary of short words I would have loved to have used at that moment, but before I could think of something more helpful or convincing, the Ohio couple returned. The wife, Janelle, was all Midwestern smiles and graciousness as she listened to the interloper laying down the law.

"Well, you know what?" Janelle said, "Since you're by yourself, I'll just bet that I can find you an even better seat, up closer. There are a few single seats I can see from here. Let's go find you one."

As the woman tentatively got up, maybe a little skeptical, Janelle asked her, "So what do you do? ... A teacher! Well, that's interesting. What's it like being a teacher? I'm a real estate agent myself."

Right before our eyes she had converted that woman into a newfound friend.

And off Janelle went, down the aisle, her hand on the arm of a person who was about to become a story we'd tell back home about how rude New Yorkers are. Right before our eyes she had converted that woman into a newfound friend. Janelle found her a better seat and when she returned I was in awe.

"THAT was amazing!"

She gave a little shrug. "I just think it was the first time anybody ever asked her what it was like to be a teacher."

Now that I had gotten out of my golden rut, synthesized happiness, gave myself permission to make some waves, and started to think like a champion, the next step was to put it all together. I wanted to define what success means to me and deal with an issue that seems to affect every entrepreneurial young person—how to balance work and life without sacrificing your goals, beliefs, or family.

CHAPTER 6: LEGACY VERSUS CURRENCY

My stack of finished books was thirty high when I chose as my next read *The Greatest Salesman In The World*, a short guide to a philosophy of living and prospering written as a parable set in pre-Christian times. It is an inspirational book that few people today have heard of because it was published nearly half a century ago and the author, Augustine "Og" Mandino, died nearly twenty years ago.

Although I wasn't that interested in parables, Mandino's messages focused on our inner lives, where those negative voices come from. He wrote about overcoming failure (his journey began when he was contemplating suicide) and unburdening himself of negative feelings toward others.

There wasn't anything particularly ground-breaking

in it but I was fascinated to learn that Mandino wrote the book because, like me, he was stuck in a negative place and decided to read a stack of self-help books. He read hundreds and, like me, wrote his own. Mandino went on to write many more books that have been published in dozens of languages. Reading saved his life. It was enriching mine.

As I got further and further into my year of reading and could feel myself growing, I began urging others to try it themselves: "You don't have to read fifty books, but reading will make you grow as a person and become a more helpful leader."

 **As I got further and further into my year of reading I could feel myself growing and began urging others to try it themselves.**

The next book after *Greatest Salesman* became one of my top favorites—*The Go-Giver: A Little Story About A Powerful Business Idea* by Bob Burg and John David Mann. Published in 2007, it also is told in parable fashion. What appealed to me was its focus on such a simple and successful way of thinking, yet most people never get it. It's as simple as what Mom and Dad told you at Christmas—'tis better to give than to receive, when you probably thought, "Yeah, right, okay, whatever. So, what DID Santa bring me this year, anyway?"

The main character in *The Go-Giver* is a consultant

named Pindar. At one point he tells the ambitious young man he's mentoring, "There's nothing wrong with making money. Lots of it, in fact. It's just not a goal that will make you successful."

It fit perfectly with my experience. My pursuit of financial success—striving toward, achieving, and then losing my status as number one in the company sales rankings—had led to dissatisfaction, boredom, and an extra twenty-five pounds. As I read, I was creating a new definition for success. As one writer put it, I stopped worrying about currency and started focusing on legacy. Success was when I invested time in a new office or branch manager, sharing what I was learning, and they ran with it, like the guy in an earlier chapter who wrote to me that he dreamed about failure.

> ## Success was when I invested time in a new office or branch manager, sharing what I was learning, and they ran with it.

Part of my growth as a leader was learning to better identify candidates who were eager, had heart, were good listeners, and had potential that could be unlocked. As the months rolled by, and then a year, and then a second year, my investments in them began to pay off. My division's sales doubled, which meant everyone, including myself, made more money.

More money, however, was not the goal. Making it was not the success. The success was watching people grow and have them come back to me a few months, a year, or two years later to tell me that something they learned on my watch made a positive difference in their lives. This was one of the threads that seemed to weave itself through almost all the books I read: If you want to receive, start by giving.

In *The Go-Giver,* Pindar tells the young man, "The majority of people operate with a mindset that says to the fireplace, 'First give me some heat, then I'll throw on some logs.' Or that says to the bank, 'Give me interest on my money, then I'll make a deposit.' And of course, it just doesn't work that way."

That describes nearly every human interaction. For it to be successful, there has to be trust. For there to be trust there has to be integrity, which is something you earn rather than simply have. So the place to start is to always be giving value to others, whether it is material, emotional, or spiritual.

Giving value to others is easy when it becomes habit.

That's what I do now, and that's what I preach. Giving value to others is easy when it becomes habit. My kids know my spiel by heart. "If you step over trash on the trail to the fish pond without picking it up, it's the same as if you put it there." But it's about more than picking up other people's trash; it's about Leaving It Better. In every talk I include some mention of my Leave It Better philosophy.

During a sales meeting at a hotel one time I was walking up an inclined hallway and noticed a maid straining to push a big cart piled high with fresh folded linens up the ramp. Barely breaking stride, I swerved toward her. "Here, let me help out." I ignored her protest, "Oh, you don't have to do that," and pushed the cart all the way to the top. Then I continued on my way.

"Thank you, sir," she called after me.

I like to tell this anecdote not because of what it says about me but what it says about all of us. How many people had walked up that busy hallway, right past that maid, and ignored her, didn't even see her, or thought about helping but hesitated? Probably a couple dozen.

It was a small moment of excitement for me, a chance to leave that maid's day just a little bit better than it was. I always feel the endorphins being released when I have an opportunity like that to put a smile on someone's face or help at an awkward or downtrodden moment. In my life so far I have probably given a few thousand dollars to homeless people I see on the street. I don't go around handing out money, but sometimes my heart tells me that doing so will leave things a little better for someone that day.

I always feel the endorphins being released when I have an opportunity to put a smile on someone's face.

During my lifetime I hope to donate a million dollars to charity. One that's close to my heart is research into the causes and solutions for people with dyslexia, a learning disability that causes people of normal or even above-average intelligence to have trouble sounding out, spelling, reading, and writing words.

Some studies suggest as many as twenty percent of the population may be affected, but few teachers know much about dyslexia. As a result, a lot of smart students get frustrated, score poorly on tests and exercises, get teased by other students, and think of themselves as too dumb to learn. It's believed that dyslexia is the number-one reason kids drop out of school. Only recently have schools in some states started screening kindergarten and first grade students for it. It makes a big difference in how successful a child will be if it can be caught early. My hope is that one day, this type of screening will be offered in every school for every child.

My education in dyslexia came about because my daughter was having so much trouble keeping up with the other kids in her class. In second grade she asked me one day, "Daddy, why can't I read as well as everybody else?" It was a heart-breaking question at the time because we didn't know.

Thousands of dollars in testing fees later, we understood what the issue was and were able to get her into tutoring programs that would help her work with her dyslexia. Today she is excelling in her reading skills and will soon be caught up to her peers in reading and writing.

There are several scientifically proven methods for teaching children with dyslexia how to improve their reading, writing, and spelling. The best of these is the Orton-Gillingham approach, which focuses on the learning needs of the individual student. This is the approach we're using with our daughter, where she is tutored one-on-one twice a week. But this level of tutoring and education is simply not available to children in need unless they are diagnosed, which is why early dyslexia screening for all children is so crucial.

In the process of helping my daughter, I learned some interesting things about dyslexia. While people with dyslexia have trouble with reading and writing words, they are often great at visual thinking, problem solving, and communicating verbally with others. They tend to be quite creative, with many dyslexics going on to careers in acting, the arts, cooking, and design. Their spatial relations skills give them an advantage in the fields of engineering, architecture, physics, and math.

I was amazed to learn that many very successful people have dyslexia and went on to personal and professional success. They include entertainers like Jim Carrey and Kiera Knightley, at least two Nobel laureates in the sciences, Virgin Group founder Richard Branson, the noted lawyer David Boies, and numerous historical figures.

It is gratifying to see that something that is typically written off as just adversity to overcome actually provides advantages as well. That's why I give as much as I can donate toward dyslexia causes.

If you've ever done something like the examples I've given, it's probable you felt that same rush of endorphins I do after leaving it better for someone. When it comes to money, there is no question that people are happier giving money away or spending it on someone else than they are spending it on themselves. That was the finding of Elizabeth Dunn and Michael Norton, co-authors of *Happy Money: The Science Of Smarter Spending.*

In a TED Talk titled "How To Buy Happiness," Norton described an experiment they conducted in Vancouver, British Columbia. They offered people who were out walking in the city an envelope that contained a five-dollar bill or a twenty-dollar bill and instructions. Some were told to spend it on themselves and others were instructed that they had to spend it on someone else. They also conducted the same experiment in Rwanda, one of the poorest countries in Africa.

The results were the same—people who spent the money on others reported being happier than they were before and people who had to spend it on themselves were no happier than before. And the amount that was spent on others made no difference. Five dollars bought just as much happiness as twenty.

Spending money on others makes people feel happier. Spending on themselves does not.

Leaving it better—giving value to others—includes small kindnesses or thoughtful gestures that cost nothing but benefit another. I was at a dinner event one night, talking to someone at the table about the meal and how the salmon had been prepared. My dinner companions seemed genuinely interested in food and in salmon in particular, especially a recipe I mentioned using. The next time I was in front of my computer I looked up my signature cedar plank salmon recipe (with brown sugar, canola oil, thyme, and cayenne pepper) and sent them an email with the link.

The high end of giving value to others might be offering to mentor someone who's struggling. In between, it can be any number of small acts that show other people that you have something of value you're willing to share with them. If you want to receive support for your dreams, start by giving support to someone else's dreams. If you want to receive encouragement in your career, start by giving encouragement to others.

If you want to receive support for your dreams, start by giving support to someone else's dreams.

Thanks to social and professional platforms like Facebook and LinkedIn, connecting with new people who could be customers or helpful in your career has become as simple as pushing a button. Anyone with an active profile on LinkedIn these days constantly receives invitations to connect from people they've never met, even though LinkedIn specifically says you should only connect with people you've known or done business with. Many recipients will delete those invitations from strangers with an annoyed growl, and some will hold it against the sender. Instead of building connections, bridges may be getting burned.

This is not networking, a term that is overused, worn out, and widely misunderstood. What many people think of as networking is often the opposite. For example, it's the opposite of networking to go to a Chamber of Commerce meeting, harvesting business cards from people you don't know, loading their emails into your address book, and sending them email messages promoting your services or products or sharing your résumé. You may have been in the same room as they were the night before, but spam is still spam. I have nothing against networking events, but you should only consider that a connection was made with people you've had a meaningful conversation with.

Networking is not about what others can do for you. It's about what you can do for others.

Networking is not about what others can do for you. It's about what you can do for others. It's just common sense. Why would someone help you unless you've already demonstrated that you're interested in helping them? If you want to have some fun with this, the next time you go to the dry cleaners or get your car serviced or just meet someone interesting at a party, ask them, "How can I help you in your business or career?"

From my experience, most people are startled at first, but asking the question often starts a conversation during which you learn something about the other person and they learn something about you. In our company, we work with people who often think they are too young and too inexperienced to offer much of anything to anyone. We teach them that just by getting to know what other people are doing, thinking about, and in need of, they'll quickly find that what they have to offer is the chance to connect them with others.

They might meet someone who's working as a realtor just when they learn that another connection is getting ready to sell a house. They might meet a young business consultant after they've connected with an entrepreneur who needs help with a business plan.

The adventure of networking is never knowing where it might lead. It's common, for example, for our reps to be offered jobs by people who've bought our knives from them. Nothing impresses like a well-executed sales presentation.

So, if business were a video game, to get the gold coins and the magic swords that will slay the dragons, you first have to help someone else prosper or solve a problem.

All of this sounds great in theory but in practice it can be frustrating for young managers who, in their enthusiasm, believe that they can fix everybody, or they can save everybody ... at first anyway. When someone on their team throws in the towel, they question whether they really can "get anybody to do this." I was that manager at one point, until I had to ask myself a tough question: Is it that some candidates are not good enough to be in my training, or is it that I'm not good enough to train them?

One of the most valuable outcomes from what I was learning and putting into practice was a mission statement that I worked with my team to create for our division. We went through the same process I had, writing down core values and then winnowing the list to the three that felt like the most important. I'm proud of what we came up with. It reflects the yearning of younger generations today who are more interested in making a difference than making a fortune. Because it was a team effort, everyone bought in to it.

I offer it here in the hopes it will stimulate you to come up with your own, or that you will find elements you can borrow.

Mission Statement, Vector Marketing,
Pennsylvania/New Jersey Division

1. Our purpose is to serve society by offering students an experience that will catapult them towards their future dreams; arming them with the success traits necessary to make a positive and meaningful impact on the world.

2. We will act and think like champions, strive to make improvements to all we embark on; leaving people, places, and the things we come in contact with better than before.

3. We will remain committed to personal and professional growth, strengthening our core values of Integrity, Balance, and Innovation.

You will notice there is nothing in our mission statement about sales targets, profits, success, or happiness. I'm a fan of the Rat Pack, a group of actors popular in the 1960s that included Frank Sinatra, Dean Martin, and Sammy Davis, Jr. Davis once said, "The manic pursuit of success cost me everything I could love: my wife, my three children, some friends I would have liked to grow old with." Take a lesson from him to heart: It's best to come by success naturally, while keeping your life in balance, rather than ruthlessly pursuing it as your only objective.

You might be asking yourself, What does being a good person, helping other people, and dedicating oneself to a cause have to do with sales and marketing?

One answer I like comes from Simon Sinek, who wrote a ground-breaking book in 2009 that helped explain why companies like Apple become so successful when what they do—make computers—is pretty much a commodity, the same thing that all their competitors do. What makes the cult of Apple tick?

Great leaders and innovators create great companies because they start out knowing why they're doing it.

In *Start With Why: How Great Leaders Inspire Everyone To Take Action*, Sinek broke it down. He decided that great leaders and innovators create great companies because they start out knowing why they're doing it.

Sinek explained the why of Steve Jobs and Apple as, "We believe that everything we do should challenge the status quo by thinking differently. How we challenge the status quo is by making products that are beautifully designed and user-friendly. And, by the way, we just happen to make computers."

Focusing on why, says Sinek, is successful because, "we prefer to do business with people who believe what we believe." We also prefer to work with people who believe what we do, which is how Google became so successful. And we prefer to follow leaders who believe what we believe. "Rev. Martin Luther King said, 'I have a dream,'" notes Sinek. "He didn't say, 'I have a plan.'"

In my business, we also sell products that are made by many competitors. Although I didn't think of it that way at the time, my year of reading books was a search for my personal why, which helped me express the why of Vector.

We believe in giving young people the experience and tools to live successful and fulfilling lives, and instilling in them the passion to help others do the same.

How we do this is by making products that are beautiful, well-designed, and meticulously crafted.

And, by the way, we just happen to sell knives.

CHAPTER 7: IS THIS A $1,400 DAY?

A story that appeared in the *Wall Street Journal* many years ago has stayed with me ever since I read it, so much so that I often use it in my talks with district managers to remind them about the big picture. It's instructive on many levels.

Carol Lees was a college freshman studying music in the 1960s when she was diagnosed with Gaucher disease, a rare degenerative condition that swells internal organs and weakens bones. There was no treatment for it at the time and the prognosis was that she might live another ten years, most of them in constant pain. What would you do in her shoes?

She went back to school with this death sentence hanging over her, struggling to find meaning in the life she had left.

She went to see a psychologist who, listening as she told her story, tried to decide whether it would be better to help her "accept the inevitable or defeat the inevitable." Carol struck him as having a survivor personality so he advised her to continue with her music. Ten years is a long time and scientists find solutions all the time for previously incurable or untreatable diseases.

Twenty-five years later, in 1991, Carol Lees was not only alive, but married with a solid career in the entertainment business, including four years running Madonna's production company. During this entire time she had sporadic bouts of fever and pain but somehow managed to keep her diagnosis a secret from everyone but her husband, who loved her so much he once proposed a suicide pact if and when she decided she could take it no more.

In spite of outliving her prognosis, Carol had that fixed-mindset voice in her head—you have an incurable disease that's going to kill you. At one point she even tried to drive her husband away to spare him the stress and grief of her inevitable passing. She wouldn't plan vacations and resisted buying a house. It became so much a part of her thinking that she even bought small sizes of toiletries.

Carol had that fixed-mindset voice in her head—you have an incurable disease that's going to kill you.

Carol had been taking part in drug trials, and when she was forty-four years old she started taking a new drug that had been developed and tested for Gaucher and found to be effective. Carol had gotten a second chance, although she still had bouts of fever and her bones had become so brittle a hug from her husband once broke a rib.

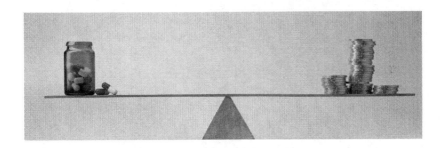

With all her problems, the biggest psychological issue for Carol became guilt about the cost of her treatments—$600,000 a year, potentially rising to $1 million. Not only were the deductible expenses of the life-saving treatment bankrupting the Lees, the cost was even bankrupting the small health insurance fund run by the writers' union she belonged to. Government subsidies and benefits made up the difference.

She calculated that her illness had cost altogether about $7 million by the time the article appeared in 2005, including multiple surgeries to replace her worn-out joints. And it was only going to get worse. Keeping her alive cost on average $1,400 a day.

She was grateful for the extra life she had been granted, but the cost started to bother her so much that she asked her husband one day, "Do I have any right to consume such a large percentage of the health-care dollars in this country? Many people would say I'm being greedy—and they would be right."

He assured her, "It's not your fault the medicine costs so much."

What Carol Lees said that kind of took my breath away when I read it, and has echoed in my thoughts so many times since, was this: "I often look around and ask myself, 'Is this a $1,400 day?' Many times, I'm not sure."

It was easy to imagine feeling that way, asking yourself, What did I do today to deserve such a staggering investment?

That was ten years ago and, incredibly, Carol Lees was alive and kicking as of May 2015, still married to her husband of more than four decades. Although she hasn't written a book about her experiences and has not been in the limelight since that *Wall Street Journal* article, I have to believe that she has been an inspiration to many people who have faced similar lifelong health issues.

In telling her story to the young managers on my teams, I want to challenge them to ask themselves whether the next twenty or so years of their lives will be worth millions to society. If you woke up every day knowing it cost somebody $1,400 to keep you going for the next twenty-four hours— every day, day in and day out—would you live your life differently? Would you be as grateful as Carol Lees? And even though you don't have a disease that costs a fortune, shouldn't you try to make every day a $1,400 day?

Shouldn't you try to make every day a $1,400 day?

Reading all those books had a dramatic effect on our division's business. My team started to make great strides when I stopped worrying about my skill as a leader and started concentrating on helping my managers develop their ability to lead and to inspire. In my talks since then I emphasize the point that the confidence and encouragement they give to each of their team members will overflow into the lives of all the other people that person interacts with, and so on—the butterfly effect. Even the smallest act ripples out into the world.

This is a lesson that takes a while to learn for many people who get promoted into their first management roles. Young leaders often get caught up in being, acting, and dressing the role as they imagine it ought to be. Leaders who are feeling insecure (we all do at one time or another) protect themselves by hiding their fears and trying to create an aura of omniscience and authority that they may not have earned yet, or that comes across as abrasive and insincere. In the process, they lose their authenticity and thus their effectiveness.

The wisdom I was picking up from the books gave me the courage to incorporate more stories from my personal life into my business life and to be more open. It wasn't in my shy nature to stand in front of a group of people who

I wanted to see me as a role model and admit that I had lost my way. But once I started talking about my crisis and what I was doing about it, I felt more confident because the people I was speaking to started to open up about themselves.

As I became more authentic, so did my team members. They began to acknowledge their own insecurities and their own negative voices. That created opportunities for me to help them sort things out and to avoid crises. The deeper I got into that year, the more borrowed wisdom I had to share, and the more people who came to rely on me for encouragement and support. We were all learning from each other and growing as a team.

In one of the books I read, *Fierce Conversations: Achieving Success At Work And In Life One Conversation At A Time* by Susan Scott, the author wrote, "It takes a certain fearlessness to make your private thoughts public. But if what you're thinking makes you squirm and wish to wriggle away, you are probably onto something."

An author whose books I did not read that year but whose work has become influential in the field of personal development is Brené Brown, a researcher who studies vulnerability, courage, authenticity, and shame. Her first book, *The Gifts Of Imperfection: Let Go Of Who You Think You're Supposed To*

Be and Embrace Who You Are, is still a best-seller, and her TED Talk on the subject has been viewed millions of times.

Brown, a self-described perfectionist, has done more than a decade of research that dispels the cultural myth that vulnerability is a weakness. "We are led to believe that if we could only look perfect and lead perfect lives, we'd no longer feel inadequate. So most of us perform, please, and perfect, all the while thinking, What if I can't keep all of these balls in the air? What will people think if I fail or give up? When can I stop proving myself?"

The culture of the workplace encourages people to hide or suppress their fears and anxiety.

We all feel vulnerable about something most of the time, but the culture of the workplace encourages people to hide or suppress their fears and anxiety. The resulting behavior can be bizarre at times, even at the highest levels as discovered by Phillip E. Rosner, a business consultant who was asked to help resolve a dispute between two departments at a Fortune 100 telecom company.

In a book about successful people whose first real job as a teenager was at a McDonald's, Rosner remembered that in the restaurant teamwork was everything. The mantra was, "If you can lean, you can clean": if you had the time to rest, you should be cleaning. The operation depended on each member pitching in when and where it was needed, without having to be asked.

The big telecom company, his client, was having trouble getting two teams of about fifteen people each to coordinate on a large project. It was causing delays and costing money. Rosner interviewed the teams and discovered that one of them was overloaded with work and missing deadlines while the other had several people twiddling their thumbs with nothing to do.

He asked the head of the slack team, "Why didn't you ask the other guy if he could use a couple of your people to help?" He looked at Rosner like he'd just said the dumbest thing in the world. To make that happen, the executive explained, would have required submitting a requisition request to the home office for permission. That might raise a question about his team being overstaffed and leave him vulnerable to a staffing cut or questions about his management abilities.

If the requisition was approved it would create work tracking hours and filling out forms detailing the time those loaners worked for the other team. This way, any added expense wouldn't show up in his budget numbers and, again, make him vulnerable to criticism.

Rosner was amazed. "I had to explain this concept of teamwork to these well-paid managers at this huge corporation and they reacted as if it was the first time they were learning this lesson—something I'd learned when I was sixteen years old at McDonald's."

Many of the books I read were about successful entrepreneurs who learned the hard way that profit without purpose is often unsustainable and definitely unsatisfying. The entrepreneur had a fixed point of view and a fixed idea about his or her role. They forgot, or never developed, the why of the business, leaving no room for collaboration, new ideas, and growth.

That's what happened to Gerald M. Levin, a CEO of Time Warner years ago who, without consulting his board of directors, arranged a merger with AOL that was such a bad idea it remains one of the biggest business failures in history. By the time it was over, $160 billion in value had burned to the ground. CNBC dubbed Levin "Worst CEO of All Time."

His story was featured in *The Dharma of Capitalism*, a book about business ethics by Nitesh Gor, a consultant in the UK who was born into a Hindu family in India. Gor draws on Hindu and Buddhist principles to make the case that our inner motivations tend to drive every decision we make and it's a good idea to gut-check your motivations before making the big ones.

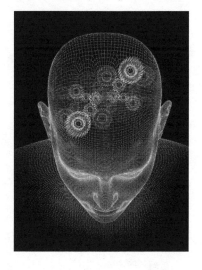

If your inner motivation is to make a name for yourself as the CEO who created the first multimedia conglomerate—like Levin, who later admitted his "messianic zeal"—chances are you're headed down the wrong track. There's no why there, just the pursuit of personal bragging rights.

The breakthrough out of my malaise reminded me of a professor I had in college who played a mind game on my philosophy class that challenged everybody's fixed mindset. In a school where most professors wore suits and ties, philosophy professor Howard Congdon was a delightful eccentric. He would occasionally show up looking like he had just rolled around in the dirt, and he was known for throwing an epic party at the end of each semester at his house. He had a brilliant mind and a great sense of humor.

One day he spent an entire class proving to all of us that there was no God. As someone who grew up going to church (but hadn't been in years) and who had never given the non-existence of God a lot of thought, it was an unnerving experience. He was convincing. At the end of the lecture I felt as if my beliefs had been badly dented, if not shattered.

As soon as I got home, I called one of my fraternity brothers who I knew was a regular church goer and asked him if he would take me to church. That was reassuring, but I kind of dreaded Professor Congdon's next lecture. What other institutions would he tear down?

 I used to be very opinionated. If you didn't totally agree with me I thought there was something wrong with you.

Instead, he spent the entire next session quoting from the Bible and other religious sources, proving that there is a God. It was an unforgettable lesson, a moment of revelation that sparked my curiosity and interest in philosophy. Up until that point I had been very opinionated, so much so that if you didn't totally agree with me I thought there was something wrong with you. Professor Congdon's lesson helped cure me of that and helped me become the leader I am today.

CHAPTER 8: ABOUT THE MONEY THING

Up to this point I've focused on the psychology behind motivation, inspiration, and success. In the several years since I immersed myself in inspirational books, my efforts to pass on some of the knowledge and wisdom I've been exposed to has been a big win for everyone.

But when it comes to the end result of all this insight and brilliance—getting paid well, especially for twenty-somethings—there's a lot of work to do. It breaks my heart a little every time I hear that one of the people I've mentored and prepared for life as an entrepreneur has made a hash of his or her prosperity. It makes me sad when people I care about unnecessarily lose money they earned, and it's bad for business. Spending more than you earn and making up the difference on credit cards gives you a negative inner voice that makes it tougher to focus on business or family.

I know how it works because I've been there and done that. I joined the company in college because I discovered that I love being an independent business person. Like most entrepreneurs, I lived paycheck to paycheck throughout my early and mid-twenties.

At that age, when you find yourself for the first time depositing checks for thousands of dollars in commissions, it doesn't take long to think up cool stuff you'd like to buy or do. For my twenty-third birthday, I bought a Toyota MR2, a sexy white two-seater with a T-top. The car dealership was delighted to arrange 100 percent financing—no money down. I drove off the lot feeling like I had arrived and allowed myself a moment of pity for some of my unfortunate peers who toiled away in fast-food restaurants for minimum wage.

Well, I lived and worked in an area with snowy winters, and the car was basically undrivable in bad weather. So I went out and leased a Nissan four-wheel-drive Pathfinder SUV. That way, I would always be able to get to my appointments but still had the option of zipping around in the MR2 when the weather was good.

My combined payments for the two vehicles came to

more than $800 a month, more than the rent on my apartment.

Humvees were all the rage in those days and when I started seeing them at traffic lights, I realized my suburban-looking Pathfinder didn't seem so tough anymore. So I went back to the dealer and traded up for a silver Hummer H2. It was like driving a presidential limo. It was always the tallest vehicle in traffic so I really felt like a king of the road.

I'd always catch a wave from other H2 drivers. There weren't all that many. People driving other cars noticed me too, usually with a middle-finger salute. I did love that truck, though. The price was $65,000, which seemed like a good deal because it weighed over 6,000 pounds, and I was able to write it off as a business expense. Nothing could have convinced me that I hadn't made a great decision.

Like most of my peers, my father rarely talked to me about money and when he did, I didn't listen. It wasn't until my late twenties, when I was thinking about getting married and settling down, that I realized how much debt I had accumulated. Since I didn't want to start a family in a financial hole, I finally buckled down and got everything paid off.

It wasn't until my late twenties that I realized how much debt I had accumulated.

I set some financial goals, started reading books and magazines about money, and talked to a financial advisor. The biggest lesson I learned: you have the power of choice. With every dollar you make, you potentially increase the power you have to choose your future. You can choose to live a few paychecks away from financial ruin or to get financially fit. It's all about choosing the right habits.

Being an entrepreneur implies being independent, but to be truly independent and not live for that next paycheck requires becoming un-dependent on credit cards and other borrowings to support the lifestyle you think you deserve or expect. It's hard to get a degree these days without ending up in debt, but the money you borrowed to get your education was an investment in your life that will pay off personally and professionally for years to come. The rest is self-indulgent stuff, which scientific research proves does not make you happier.

> **The money you borrowed to get your education was an investment in your life. The rest is self-indulgent stuff.**

Being un-dependent does make you happier when you have the opportunity to help those you love. During my first summer out of college, I went to visit my mother on her birthday. She'd been recently laid off and had fallen two months behind with her rent. She was in real danger of being evicted. I went to her landlord, got her caught up, and put the receipt in a birthday card.

My mother burst into tears when she opened it. My eyes flooded as well. I had never felt as independent as I did in that moment, but I was also so grateful that I could give back for all the sacrifices I knew she'd made for me. I'd have felt terrible if, instead, all my spare cash had gone to support a fancy car or a credit card bill for sports jerseys and nights on the town.

One of the books I read was *The Total Money Makeover* by Dave Ramsey, a radio talk-show host. It was so good that I've officially incorporated Ramsey's program into our training for our new assistant and branch managers. The key to successfully managing your money, he says, is something he calls gazelle intensity. Live your financial life the way a gazelle saves itself from an attacking cheetah: "Outmaneuver the enemy and run for your life!"

If you recognize yourself as someone who has lost control of your money, not having enough left over after paying the bills, in debt and wanting to get out, or just confused about what you should be doing with your money, Ramsey's book is a good start. And don't feel bad, because people of all ages are confused about how money and interest rates work. And who can blame anyone for being confused about taxes since the laws are thousands of pages long and the rules change from year to year.

Don't feel bad. People of all ages are confused about how money and interest rates work.

In his book, *Take Back Your Money*, investment advisor John E. Girouard explains some basic principles of smart money management, beginning with two really insightful pieces of advice. First, before anything else, put away an emergency fund of at least six months of your expenses, just in case your good-paying job doesn't work out.

Although some experts disagree, I personally don't believe in saddling yourself with car payments and I believe you should pay off your mortgage in fifteen years or less. If you're worried about losing the mortgage interest deduction, you can donate what you would have paid in interest to charity, write it off, and feel good about "leaving it better." More on the details later, but here's a segment from Girouard's book that might make a young person feel a little less dumb about money.

If you are on the younger side of life, in your twenties and thirties, you may see a well-dressed

TAKE BACK YOUR MONEY

older couple drive by in an expensive car and conclude that they are financially independent. You think how great it must be to be rich and have so many choices. You might be surprised to learn that a fair number of the people who look rich are in hock to their eyebrows, enslaved by investments that aren't working out, or may be truly wealthy but live in terror of losing what they've gained. Many financial professionals have a story that is a variation on the widow who inherited several million dollars yet complained that she couldn't afford to go with her friends on their cruise vacations. Your brain can turn out some odd notions when it comes to money.

You also might be surprised to learn that the well-dressed couple who drove past you in their expensive car might look at you in your ten-year-old compact sedan, which you bought with the money saved doing freelance work on weekends, and sigh with envy because they think your life is so much simpler than theirs. They might be surprised to learn that you're in hock to your eyebrows with college loans, your credit cards are maxed out, and you had to move back home because you couldn't afford the rent on your apartment.

You might both be on your way to bankruptcy court.

In the next chapter I'll lay out the steps that, if followed, will help you get a handle on your financial life and start enjoying the independent feeling of knowing that your hard-earned dollars are working for you and not someone else.

In addition to Ramsey's excellent *Total Money Makeover* and Girouard's *Take Back Your Money*, another book that's popular is *Get A Financial Life: Personal Finance In Your Twenties And Thirties* by Beth Kobliner. Your financial concerns are not the same as your parents' or your grandparents', so Kobliner focuses on the stuff many students are dealing with, like college loans and how to start saving.

Finally, there are some excellent, thought-provoking TED Talks by social scientists who have studied how people feel about money and the relationship between money and happiness. A list of books and a few of the outstanding TED Talks are in the Appendix at the back of this book.

CHAPTER 9: MONEY, THE USER MANUAL

When I decided I needed to include a financial component to our training, and after reading Dave Ramsey's book, *The Total Money Makeover*, I invested a few hundred dollars on his Foundations in Personal Finance College Edition, a DVD course. I did it mainly to see if it might be effective for my district managers, and hoped to learn a few tips along the way, although by this time I had pretty much locked down my own financial life. My wife and I have no credit card debt, no car payments, an emergency fund, and are on track to pay off our house in fifteen years or less.

I was impressed and introduced it to my team members, some of whom were talking about it being a life-changing experience just halfway through the first lesson. My personal goal is to spin off more future self-made millionaires than any other company in the world. I can't make people act, but at least they'll know how to do it.

The following is a thumbnail sketch of the steps that should help you on your journey to financial freedom.

1) CREATE A WRITTEN GAME PLAN

This is budgeting 101. Every month you track of all your expenses, ideally in a spreadsheet, Quicken, or Mint.com. Don't forget to include a category for savings. Most people think this is a once a month task but most successful people look at their budget weekly, or even twice a week.

This was a mistake I made more than once in my early years. I'd get to the end of the month and wonder, How did I get here? What happened?

Keeping track of your expenses weekly will help avoid surprises. After teaching thousands of students about how to win with money over the past two decades, I've found that most people navigate their financial lives by looking in the rearview mirror instead of at the road ahead.

Log in your expenditures twice a week and re-evaluate where you are. This way you can course correct before you end up stranded on the Isle of Someday—Someday I'll get a grip on my finances; Someday I'll save for retirement; Someday I'll work on my budget.

2) ACT YOUR WAGE

As Ramsey puts it, "You have to live on less than you make. You are not in Congress."

While I did have a blast at times living beyond my means, my wife reminds me that we didn't really enjoy living that way, paycheck to paycheck, in order to drive fancy cars, buy expensive clothes, furniture, etc., that we have since had to replace, and in general keeping up with the pseudo-rich. It added unnecessary stress to our already hectic lives.

Living on borrowed money is what most people have been doing, but all you need do is talk to some Baby Boomers to know what that's done to their retirement plans. It's much easier to save money when you aren't paying for your lifestyle with money you *expect* to earn.

3) GET AND STAY OUT OF DEBT

At one point in my twenties I had six different credit cards to keep track of, so six different payments had to be made on time. Had I continued I would have been destined to work for Visa, Discover, MasterCard, and American Express forever. No payments means no distraction.

According to Dave Ramsey's book, three out of four of the wealthiest Americans said the number one way to become wealthy is to get and stay out of debt—no car payments, no student loans, no credit card payments.

If you already have debt, it's time to make a plan. Put it all into a spreadsheet and get to work. There are several versions of the debt repayment plan that Ramsey calls the

Debt Snowball. You either start by paying off the debt that has the highest interest rate or the one with the smallest balance. The second one is my preference because it sets you up for a quick win that will help keep you motivated.

Ramsey suggests paying the minimum installment on every account except the one with the smallest balance, which you should attack with any extra money you have. Once that debt is gone, do the same with your next smallest balance until you've killed it off. Keep going like that.

I love Ramsey's explanation. He says it may make more sense mathematically to start with the highest interest rate first, but, "If you were good at math, you wouldn't be in this situation, now would you?" Paying off the smallest debt first gives you momentum. Set a goal to pay it off by a target date and make whatever sacrifices you can to stick to it. Eat in, work extra hours, whatever it takes, it WILL be worth it!

Set a goal to pay off all your debt, excluding mortgage and student loans, within eighteen months. If you make the commitment you'll be surprised at what you can accomplish. Your mortgage payments are not the same as credit card debt because, one way or another, you have to have a roof over your head. Unless you have enough saved to pay cash for your home, mortgage payments are a necessity. And with mortgage interest rates currently at or near long-term lows, you will be better off first putting money into an emergency fund or into a 401(k) that will defer some taxes and get you in the habit of building a real retirement fund.

The risk in paying off a mortgage on your principal residence is that in the event of a serious health or income emergency, you may not be able to get that money back out of the house when you need it.

4) SAVE YOURSELF

Once you're out of debt (except the mortgage), the next step is an emergency fund. According to most experts, you'll want at least three months of your household expenses in a savings or money market account. Six months is ideal, but three will get you started.

Look at your necessary household expenses, the ones you would still have to meet if you lost your job. Imagine how much calmer and rational you'd be if you did lose your job or were unable to work for some reason. You'd have no debt or car payments, and six months of expenses in cash.

Once you have your rainy day fund filled up, start saving for the things you want or will eventually need to purchase. Now that you have no car payments, you can save that same amount each month so when it comes time to buy another car, you'll be able to pay cash instead of borrowing.

How about the twenty-year roof you've got on your fourteen-year-old house? You should be saving for it so that in six years you won't have to borrow to replace it.

Finally, save for wealth building. It's easier than you think because of a wonderful thing called compound interest, which has been called the eighth wonder of the world. "He who understands it, earns it," the saying goes, "and he who doesn't pays it."

The simplest illustration of how compound interest works is one that's fun to describe to kids. It's theoretical but it leaves a big impression.

If I give you a penny today and promise to pay you 100 percent interest every day (your balance doubles every day), and you don't take any money out for a month, how much will you have at the end of thirty days? How about $10,737,418.24?

The same math works with credit card debt—you're paying interest on interest.

So, when saving for retirement, consider this calculation. If you invested $100 per month in a Roth IRA (which grows tax free) for forty years, it's a fairly safe bet you'd end up with a retirement fund of $1 million. I'd be willing to bet anyone I know that they blew more than $100 on "stuff" in the past month, and probably can't even remember where it went. If you have a budget that you monitor weekly, you will.

5) INVEST IN YOURSELF

a) Your Home

For most people, buying a home is the largest purchase/ investment they will ever make, and usually the best vehicle for building wealth because of the mortgage interest tax deduction. I personally recommend no longer than a fifteen-year fixed-rate mortgage, although there are some financial advisors who would recommend a longer mortgage that lowers your monthly payment, BUT only if you are putting the difference into a solid investment or savings account and leaving it there.

It depends on several factors. Is this the house you expect to live in for at least ten years? You should know that the average homeowner does not stay in a house more than about ten years. Do you have the discipline to either pay your mortgage off early, or put the extra cash flow from a longer mortgage away in a lock box-style investment? Or, in your market, is it on balance cheaper to rent and sock away the money you would ordinarily spend on replacing roofs, water heaters, and other repairs? Owning a home is a smart financial move for most people, but there are pitfalls and headaches.

On the other hand, one of the common mistakes many people with a thirty-year mortgage make is refinancing periodically to pay off other debt. It could end up taking them forty years or more to pay it off and cost a lot more money.

In my opinion (see a professional!), once your fifteen-year mortgage is paid off, you're going to find wealth building to be very easy. And if you still need the tax write-off that the interest on your home gave you each year, just donate that same amount of money to charity. This way you decide who gets it instead of Congress.

If you are about to buy your first home, here is something to keep in mind. Do not buy the nicest house in the neighborhood. It won't increase in value at the same rate as the rest of the neighborhood. If you're smart, you'll look for a home that needs a little Tender Loving Care in an otherwise good neighborhood. You may be amazed at how easily new carpeting and some paint can transform a home's appearance.

b) If you are an entrepreneur, invest in your business. It's the number one investment of the affluent.

c) A Roth IRA = $5,500* per year ($6,500* if you're fifty or older) that grows tax free. As long as you wait until you are 59 and 1/2 and the money has been there for at least 5 years, you pay no taxes when you take the money out.

d) A single or Solo 401(k), also known as a Single K. You can invest up to $17,500* per year, which reduces your income taxes. See a professional to be sure which of the options is best for you.

e) A SEP (Simplified Employee Pension). You can invest 19 percent of your profit or 25 percent of your salary if you are incorporated, up to $51,000*. Ask your accountant.

f) A traditional IRA allows you to invest up to $5,500* per year ($6,500* if you're fifty or older). This is a tax-deductible investment, although you will have to pay taxes when you take it out at retirement. I strongly advise checking with your accountant about rules and options.

*As of 2015. Amounts typically increase over time.

6) INVEST IN OTHER THINGS

After maxing out your Roth or SEP or other retirement accounts:

a) Mutual funds that invest in stocks and bonds are another way to take advantage of compounding—the snowball effect that happens when your earnings generate even more earnings. The best advice is to consult an advisor who is a certified fiduciary. Fiduciaries are obligated by law to give advice in the best interest of their clients and will likely guide you to the lowest cost funds available based on your goals.

b) Certain kinds of whole life insurance include a savings account feature that, in effect, allows you to become your own bank. Investment advisors make huge commissions selling insurance policies and some are more expensive than others. Some advisors strongly suggest buying a whole life policy from a mutually owned insurance company. That's a company that is owned by the policy holders, not share-holders. Expenses are lower and how much you can earn is usually higher. Here are two resources: **bankonyourself.com** and **lifetimeincome.com**.

c) Income-producing real estate: If I had my twenties to do all over again I would buy a duplex, live in one half and rent out the other half, or buy near a college and rent each room to students, an investment I actually have made. A property with more than four units is a good way to hedge against vacancies. A book I found helpful is *The ABCs of Real Estate Investing* by Ken McElroy.

7) TO INCORPORATE OR NOT INCORPORATE

If you are an entrepreneur or self-employed, most experts advise setting yourself up as a limited liability corporation (LLC) or what's known as an S corporation, for the letter assigned by the IRS. There are lots of rules and options that a good accountant or tax attorney can help you with that might save you on taxes and could protect your assets in the event of a business disaster.

8) EVERYDAY INSURANCE

Make sure you have the right insurance so you and your family are protected. Here are the seven types of insurance that Dave Ramsey says you absolutely need.

a) Homeowner's/Renter's Insurance

b) Auto Insurance

c) Health Insurance

d) Disability Insurance

e) Long-Term Care Insurance

f) Identity Theft Protection

g) Life Insurance: Term life insurance is the most affordable and is intended for short-term protection for your family for the unexpected. The price goes up each year as you get older.

9) YOUR COMMUNITY

Scientifically, people who give money to charity are happier than those who spend all their money on themselves. But you can be generous in many smaller ways, like paying for the person's coffee behind you in line or buying a homeless person a hot meal. And you don't need to give money to be generous. You can give your time. There are so many charities in need of volunteers. You can even give blood. You could collect and donate unwanted clothing, books, and household items to organizations that give them to the needy or sell them to raise funds.

CHAPTER 10: MY YEAR OF READING BOOK LIST

Below is a list of the fifty books I read as part of my year of reading challenge, listed in the order that I read them. I've tried to include a quote or message from each that I found particularly inspirational. My favorite books are marked with a double asterisk (**).

In support of my mission for personal and professional growth, Vector Marketing Corporation reimbursed me for the purchase price of all the books.

1. ** *The 4-Hour Workweek: Escape 9-5, Live Anywhere, And Join The New Rich,* Timothy Ferriss - This was the first of the books I read, which tells you where my head was at when I began! "What we fear most is usually what we most need to do."

2. ** *Love Is The Killer App: How To Win Business And Influence Friends,* Tim Sanders - This book's message and author are the reason why I continue to read and share the wisdom I learn with others. "Just as the reason we own things is to share the with others, the reason we acquire knowledge is to share it. Otherwise, we don't truly distribute love."

3. *The Tipping Point: How Little Things Can Make A Big Difference,* Malcolm Gladwell - "The values of the world we inhabit and the people we surround ourselves with have a profound effect on who we are."

4. *Inside Steve's Brain: Business Lessons From Steve Jobs, The Man Who Saved Apple,* Leander Kahney - "The way you motivate people is to get them into your product, to entertain them, and to turn your product into an incredibly important event."

5. ** *Pour Your Heart Into It: How Starbucks Built A Company One Cup At A Time,* Howard Schultz and Dori Jones Yang - This book powerfully reminded me that I needed to work on me in order to be a great business leader. "You can't build a hundred-story skyscraper on a foundation designed for a two-story house." "One of the fundamental aspects of leadership is the ability to instill confidence in others when you yourself are feeling insecure."

6. *Think Like A Champion: An Informal Education In Business And Life,* Donald Trump - "Never think

of learning as being a burden or studying as being boring. It may take some discipline, but it can be an adventure. It can prepare you for a new beginning."

7. *Outliers: The Story Of Success*, Malcolm Gladwell - This book explains the 10,000-hours rule, which posits that the key to achieving expertise in any skill comes after practicing it for at least 10,000 hours.

8. *How To Get Your Point Across In 30 Seconds Or Less*, Milo O. Frank - This book is about the importance of using a Hook to "allure, entice, tempt, tantalize, fascinate, captivate, enchant, attract, bewitch, catch, hypnotize, and make them remember" at the start of your thirty-second message.

9. *The Pursuit Of Wow!: Every Person's Guide To Topsy-Turvy Times*, Tom Peters - "Curiosity is more important than knowledge."

10. ** *Becoming A Person of Influence: How To Positively Impact The Lives Of Others*, John C. Maxwell - Everything he writes has a big impact. This book was especially packed with great lessons. "The goal of many leaders is to get people to think more highly of the leader. The goal of a great leader is to help people think more highly of themselves."

11. *Blink: The Power Of Thinking Without Thinking*, Malcolm Gladwell - "The key to good decision-making is not knowledge. It is understanding. We are swimming in the former. We are desperately lacking in the latter."

12. *Fierce Conversations: Achieving Success At Work And In Life One Conversation At A Time,* Susan Scott - "As a leader, you get what you tolerate. People do not repeat behavior unless it is rewarded."

13. *** Crush It!: Why NOW Is The Time To Cash In On Your Passion,* Gary Vaynerchuk - This book on branding was an absolute blast to read. "True success—financial, personal, and professional—lies above all in loving your family, working hard, and living your passion. In telling your story. In authenticity, hustle, and patience. In caring fiercely about the big and small stuff. In valuing legacy over currency."

14. *What The Dog Saw: And Other Adventures,* Malcolm Gladwell - "Good writing does not succeed or fail on the strength of its ability to persuade. It succeeds or fails on the strength of its ability to engage you, to make you think, to give you a glimpse into someone elses head."

15. *The Likeability Factor: How To Boost Your L-Factor And Achieve Your Life's Dreams,* Tim Sanders - "Tonight, before you fall asleep, ask yourself, 'Have I made someone smile today?' If your answer is no, make sure that tomorrow night the answer is yes."

16. *Mentoring 101,* John C. Maxwell - "You can not give what you do not have. In order to develop your staff, you must keep growing yourself."

17. *The 21 Indispensable Qualities Of A Leader: Becoming The Person Others Will Want To Follow,* John C. Maxwell - Are you pouring your life into others? Great section on the four truths about passion.

18. *The Pixar Touch: The Making Of A Company,* David A. Price - Neat to read the behind-the-scenes story of the making of Pixar and how Steve Jobs really became a billionaire.

19. *The Leap: How 3 Simple Changes Can Propel Your Career From Good To Great,* Rick Smith - "Myth #1: To make a great change in your life, you must change who you are. Not so. You must become more completely who you already are."

20. *Outstanding! 47 Ways To Make Your Organization Exceptional,* John G. Miller - "Alignment comes from believing in the values of the organization, and then practicing those values, even when it's not convenient."

21. ** *Drive: The Surprising Truth About What Motivates Us,* Daniel H. Pink - This guided me to make my team's work more meaningful by talking more about our purpose than our profits. It also got me to get the team involved in the creation of our purpose statement.

22. *How The Mighty Fall: And Why Some Companies Never Give In,* Jim Collins - "In teaching, don't try to come up with the right answers; focus on coming up with good questions."

23. *The Definitive Guide to Body Language,* Allan Pease and Barbara Pease - Great book on pretty much everything you ever wanted to know about reading people and even on how to change your own body language to be more open when communicating and more effective on stage.

24. *Six Pixels of Separation: Everyone Is Connected. Connect Your Business to Everyone,* Mitch Joel - "Your [social media] strategy sucks (mostly because you're not thinking about it enough)."

25. *Self-Improvement 101: What Every Leader Needs To Know,* John C. Maxwell - "Growth must be intentional—nobody improves by accident."

26. *Think Better: An Innovator's Guide To Productive Thinking,* Tim Hurson - Great book on how we think and how to be a productive thinker.

27. *Attitude 101: What Every Leader Needs To Know,* John C. Maxwell - "Value people, praise effort, reward performance."

28. *Sway: The Irresistible Pull Of Irrational Behavior,* Ori Brafman and Rom Brafman - An interesting look into what derails our decision-making.

29. *The Dharma Of Capitalism: A Guide to Mindful Decision-Making In The Business Of Life,* Nitesh Gor - Great book about operating in the Mode of Goodness,

making good choices for the benefit of society and profitability, not just making decisions to get the business at any cost.

30. *Leadership 101: What Every Leader Needs To Know,* John C. Maxwell - Great chapter on influence and empowering others.

31. *The Book of FIVE RINGS,* Miyamoto Musahshi - Great book ... if I ever need to enter a sword fight I'll be ready.

32. *The Greatest Salesman in the World,* Augustine "Og" Mandino - "Failure will never overtake you if your determination to succeed is strong enough."

33. *The Go-Giver: A Little Story About A Powerful Business Idea,* Bob Burg and John David Mann - "Your true worth is determined by how much more you give in value than you take in payment."

34. *The Dream Manager,* Matthew Kelly and Patrick Lencioni - Great reminder to make sure you connect your employees' current jobs to their dreams.

35. *Sh** My Dad Says,* Justin Halpern - By far the funniest book I've read. I was in stitches. Takeaways: Don't get so caught up in what people you don't know think about you. Speak your mind.

36. *The Way of Zen,* Alan Watts - Beautiful, insightful look into Zen Buddhism.

37. *Game Warden: Adventures Of A Wildlife Warrior,* William Wasserman - "Treat all people right, even those that aren't right themselves. It's just a better way to live."

38. *The Winner's Brain: 8 Strategies Great Minds Use To Achieve Success,* Jeff Brown and Mark Fenske - This book helped me in coaching managers with decision-making and motivation. I love the idea of "single-tasking," the ability to give your undivided attention to one thing at a time.

39. ** *The Total Money Makeover: A Proven Plan For Financial Fitness,* Dave Ramsey - This book is amazing at teaching the basics of being on top of one's finances, saving, investing, getting out of debt, and building wealth. I have taught Ramsey's Foundations in Personal Finance to our Leadership Academy for the past several years now. Many people have told me his advice has been life-changing.

40. *The Accidental Billionaires: The Founding Of Facebook: A Tale Of Sex, Money, Genius And Betrayal,* Ben Mezrich - Way more entertaining than I had hoped. I couldn't put it down.

41. ** *8 Ways To Great: Peak Performance On The Job And In Your Life,* Doug Hirschhorn - This is one of the best books I've ever read. It could easily be called How To Sell A Ton Of Product On A Tight Deadline. It's got lots of great information on finding your Why and good material for coaching both sales reps and managers.

42. ** *Delivering Happiness: A Path To Profits, Passion, And Purpose,* Tony Hsieh - I'm a huge fan of the story of Zappos and of the company, which has the best customer service in America. It's the best book I've read on creating culture and core values in your business with passion and purpose.

43. *Tribes: We Need You To Lead Us,* Seth Godin - "Being charismatic doesn't make you a leader. Being a leader makes you charismatic."

44. *How Successful People Think: Change Your Thinking, Change Your Life,* John C. Maxwell - "Our thoughts determine our destiny. Our destiny determines our legacy."

45. *The Last Lecture,* Randy Pausch and Jeffrey Zaslow - "Complaining does not work as a strategy. We all have finite time and energy. Any time we spend whining is unlikely to help us achieve our goals. And it won't make us happier."

46. *Little Voice Mastery: How To Win The War Between Your Ears In 30 Seconds Or Less And Have An Extraordinary Life!,* Blair Singer - There are at least 20 coaching exercises here I can do with my team to help them build confidence and achieve peak performance.

47. *Switch: How To Change Things When Change Is Hard,* Chip Heath and Dan Heath - Excellent book on the tension between our rational and emotional minds and how to unite them for great results.

48. ** *Mindset: The New Psychology Of Success*, Carol S. Dweck - This book was hugely influential in teaching me about fixed versus growth mindset. I use a lot of this material in my motivational talks.

49. *Rework,* Jason Fried and David Heinemeier Hansson - "Interruption is the enemy of productivity. Momentum fuels motivation."

50. *The Leader Who Had No Title: A Modern Fable On Real Success In Business And Life,* Robin Sharma - "One of the best moves you can make is to methodically remove all the walls standing between you and your genius, which will lead to you becoming more intimate with your very best you."

ALSO

Here are some other books I've read outside of my year-long challenge that I've found personally and professionally helpful.

Start With Why: How Great Leaders Inspire Everyone To Take Action, Simon Sinek

"Very few people or companies can clearly articulate WHY they do WHAT they do. By WHY I mean your purpose, cause or belief —WHY does your company exist? WHY do you get out of bed every morning? And WHY should anyone care? People don't buy what you do; they buy why you do it."

You Already Know How To Be Great: A Simple Way To Remove Interference And Unlock Your Greatest Potential, Alan Fine and Rebecca R. Merrill

Fantastic book. It will teach you the G.R.O.W. technique of coaching to help your mentees find their own "Way Forward."

Bury My Heart At Conference Room B: The Unbeatable Impact Of Truly Committed Managers, Stan Slap

"Discover your core values and help others do the same."

Go-Givers Sell More, Bob Burg and John David Mann

This fun sequel to *The Go-Giver* is a practical guide on how giving is the best way to pave the path to success.

The Happiness Advantage: The Seven Principles Of Positive Psychology That Fuel Success And Performance At Work, Shawn Achor

How happiness fuels success instead of vice versa.

The 4-Hour Body: An Uncommon Guide To Rapid Fat-Loss, Incredible Sex, And Becoming Superhuman, Timothy Ferriss

Helped me lose twenty-five pounds in three months, and keep it off ever since.

Brains On Fire: Igniting Powerful, Sustainable, Word Of Mouth Movements, Robbin Phillips, Greg Cordell, Geno Church, and Spike Jones

Great book on starting a movement to ignite your team.

"As a strong leader you can start a movement. You *should* start a movement. Passion is the key to a sustainable movement. You can't have passion without purpose. There are more lessons to learn, more stories to share and more movements to ignite... So join the Movement. Let's write the next chapters together. This is just the beginning."

The Power Of Habit: Why We Do What We Do In Life And Business, Charles Duhigg

Using scientific evidence, the author explains how to understand our habits so we can change them.

The Fire Starter Sessions: A Soulful + Practical Guide To Creating Success On Your Own Terms, Danielle LaPorte

Focuses on getting clear about how we want to feel as a way to map out our work and life goals.

David And Goliath: Underdogs, Misfits, And The Art Of Battling Giants, Malcolm Gladwell

Challenges how we think about obstacles and adversity. Especially notable is chapter four, titled "You Wouldn't Wish Dyslexia On Your Child. Or Would You?"

Man's Search For Meaning, Viktor E. Frankl

This memoir about surviving the Holocaust is an essential read on how to cope with suffering and hardship, overcome it, and find meaning in life.

No Shorts, Flip-Flops, Or Sunglasses: How To Get And Make The Most Of Your First Real Job, John Wasserman

Of course I had to plug my first book, which is a fun, no-nonsense primer on the modern-day workplace for young adults.

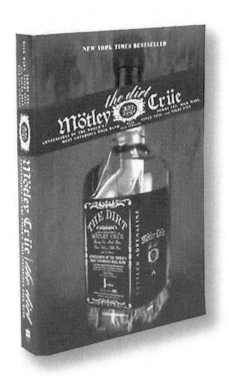

THE FIFTY-FIRST BOOK: FINAL THOUGHTS

After reading fifty books on business, leadership, and self-help, which I finished in forty-nine weeks—three weeks ahead of schedule—the habit of reading had become part of my DNA. However, the last thing I wanted to do at that time was read another self-help book.

So I picked up *The Dirt: Confessions Of The World's Most Notorious Rock Band*, the best-selling memoir by the members of Mötley Crüe, whose song "Kick Start My Heart" I had selected as the alarm on my cell phone. It helped cure my snooze bingeing.

In it guitarist Mick Mars drops three consecutive strings resulting in a sound similar to a motorcycle shifting gears. The riff that follows lives up to the song's title and will start your blood pumping. I can't help but get up and go when it kicks on.

Book Fifty-One didn't help me grow personally or professionally, and it may actually have subtracted seven or eight books from my growth that year, but it was worth it. I couldn't put it down.

APPENDIX: ADDITIONAL RESOURCES

Following are some additional resources that may be helpful to you in your own journey toward thriving.

GREAT TED TALKS

TED Talks are famous for presenting powerful and engaging ideas in twenty-minute videos. You will find these either at TED.com or by searching on YouTube.com.

Brené Brown: "The Power Of Vulnerability." This beloved TED Talk is filled with deep insights from Brown's research on how humans connect.

Barry Schwartz: "Paradox of Choice." Schwartz, a sociology professor at Swarthmore College and author of *The Paradox of Choice*, explains how and why the abundance of choice in modern society is actually making us miserable.

Michael Norton: "How To Buy Happiness." Fascinating research on how money can indeed buy happiness—when you don't spend it on yourself.

Dan Gilbert: "The Surprising Science of Happiness." Author of *Stumbling on Happiness* challenges the idea that we'll be miserable if we don't get what we want.

Graham Hill: "Less Stuff, More Happiness." A writer and designer asks if having less stuff, in less room, could lead to more happiness.

Paul Piff: "Does Money Make You Mean?" Research using a rigged game of Monopoly reveals how badly people behave and feel when they become wealthy.

Daniel Kahneman: "The Riddle of Experience vs. Memory." The Nobel laureate and founder of behavioral economics reveals how our "experiencing selves" and our "remembering selves" perceive happiness differently.

DYSLEXIA RESOURCES

Dyslexia, a neurologically based disorder that interferes with the acquisition and processing of language and that often runs in families, affects about one in five children. Early diagnosis is important so that children can get the proper education and resources to help them excel. Below are a few links with more information.

Dyslexia Training Institute: Provides education on dyslexia and interventions and classes.

www.dyslexiatraininginstitute.org/

Headstrong Nation: This site provides information for adults with dyslexia on workplace accommodations as well as pursuing entrepreneurship and professional talents with dyslexia.

www.headstrongnation.org

Children's Dyslexia Centers serves thirteen states and helped my family with our daughter's dyslexia. They provide tutoring at no charge to children from early elementary through high school who have been diagnosed as dyslexic. Children are eligible regardless of economic status. The positive impact of early intervention on the lives of these children and their families is enormous and inspires our commitment to this program.

www.childrensdyslexiacenters.org/

ADDITIONAL READING ON MONEY, FINANCES

There's no shortage of books out there on money and finances, and if you watched Barry Schwartz's TED Talk on "The Paradox Of Choice," you'll know how having so many choices of books can lead you to book-buying paralysis. A couple of my top favorites:

David Ramsey's *The Total Money Makeover: A Proven Plan For Financial Success*. This is probably your best starting point as a strong primer on spending, saving, debt, and wealth creation.

MONEY Master the Game: 7 Simple Steps to Financial Freedom, by Tony Robbins.

OTHER RECOMMENDED BOOKS

The Millionaire Next Door: The Surprising Secrets of America's Wealthy, Thomas J. Stanley and William D. Danko: Identifies seven common traits that show up again and again among those who have accumulated wealth.

Stop Acting Rich ... And Start Living Like A Real Millionaire, Thomas J. Stanley: Puts wealth in perspective and shows you how to live rich without spending more.

Rich Dad's Guide to Becoming Rich Without Cutting Up Your Credit Cards: Turn "Bad Debt" Into "Good Debt", Robert T. Kiyosaki: Kiyosaki argues that what really makes you rich is a strong financial education, not just cutting up your credit cards. He has a whole series of "Rich Dad" books on various financial subjects that are helpful.

FINANCIAL WEBSITES

When it comes to financial advice, nothing beats the help of a certified fiduciary. Fiduciaries are obligated by law to give advice in the best interest of their clients and will likely guide you to the lowest cost funds available based on your goals.

The National Association of Personal Financial Advisors (NAPFA) is the country's leading professional association of fee-only financial advisors: www.napfa.org/ or www.findanadvisor.napfa.org/home.aspx.

Fee-only financial planners are registered investment advisors. They do not accept fees or compensation based on product sales. Fee-only advisors have fewer inherent conflicts of interest, and they generally provide more comprehensive advice.

On the next page are a few websites that can help you do it yourself and keep track of spending, create a budget, pay off debt, and save money. Let me state for the record that I'm not endorsing any one site or product over another, simply providing a round-up list of some of the many sites out there. The most important thing is finding a system that you like and will use, so do some searching and trial runs until you find a site or app that appeals to you.

OVERALL FINANCIAL ADVICE

DaveRamsey.com: I find Dave Ramsey's financial advice to be some of the best around. In addition to his excellent books on personal money management, he also offers a website with articles and tools on money.

HELP MANAGING A BUDGET

Mint.com: This website helps you manage your budget. Create an account with Mint and link it to your bank accounts, credit cards, loans, and investments. By tracking every transaction you make in one place, you can better understand your spending. Also a smartphone app.

MoneyStream.com: This is another great budgeting website that detects when your bills are due, schedules them into a calendar, alerts you to unusual activity, and shows you past and future cash flow. Also a smartphone app.

Buxfer.com: This is a great site for tracking expenses. It also has a feature that allows you to track group expenses that are shared, like rent and utilities that you split with roommates. You can sync it to your bank accounts and even import information from other software like Quicken into Buxfer.

PersonalCapital.com: This site also allows you to create and manage a budget, with the added feature of allowing you to become an investment client. If you choose this option, you'll be paired with an advisor who can help with your wealth-building goals. Also a smartphone app.

LevelMoney.com: This is a simplified budgeting site. Rather than breaking down expenses into microcategories, it tracks your daily spending and keeps you updated on your bank balances. Also a smartphone app.

HELP REDUCING DEBT AND SAVING

ReadyForZero.com: This website helps you pay off debt faster by helping you create a repayment plan that fits your budget. It's useful for student loan payments, car payments, or credit card bills. Also a smartphone app.

FeedThePig.org: This is a great website for young people who want to start learning how to save more money. The site offers tips for how small changes in financial habits can make a big difference and also offers advice on how to pay down debt and make saving a habit.

SavedPlus.com: This site makes it effortless to automatically save, invest, or pay down your debts. You set it to transfer a certain amount or percentage of your money each month into a savings or other account. It includes a savings calculator so you can determine how much you should be saving for retirement. Also a smartphone app.

IMPULSE SPENDING, BUILDING CREDIT

CreditKarma.com: Your credit score can affect everything, from your ability to get a loan to even getting hired. This site offers truly free access to your credit score any time. It also offers other financial tools, like free credit monitoring and debt management. You don't need a credit card to sign up and you'll never be charged; the site is kept free via advertising. Also a smartphone app.

Hukkster.com: I encourage my employees to avoid impulse buys and save up for things they want, especially bigger or pricier purchases. This website can track items you've found online and alert you when they go on sale or when a discount code becomes available for them. Also a smartphone app.

Earmark.com: This site is billed as helping "people who hate budgeting save money while spending it." By using the app to track impulse purchases you've forgone (like an unnecessary cab ride or latte), you'll know how much money you can save for meaningful purchases like a trip or special item for your home. Also a smartphone app.